Ex Libris

Randy Manning

THE SHENANDOAH IN FLAMES
The Valley Campaign of 1864

VIRGINIA'S EMBATTLED VALLEY

In the spring of 1864, the fertile Shenandoah Valley again became a battleground. As the Army of the Potomac grappled with Robert E. Lee's Army of Northern Virginia east of the Blue Ridge Mountains, other Federals launched a campaign of destruction in the Valley, attempting to deprive Lee of his food supply. But Union General Franz Sigel was defeated at New Market in May and General David Hunter was rebuffed at Lynchburg in June. Then the Confederates took the offensive: General Jubal A. Early invaded Maryland and threatened Washington. Shaken, the Federals put U. S. Grant's personal choice, General Philip H. Sheridan, in command of the Army of the Shenandoah, setting the stage for a confrontation that would climax in the Battle of Cedar Creek on October 19.

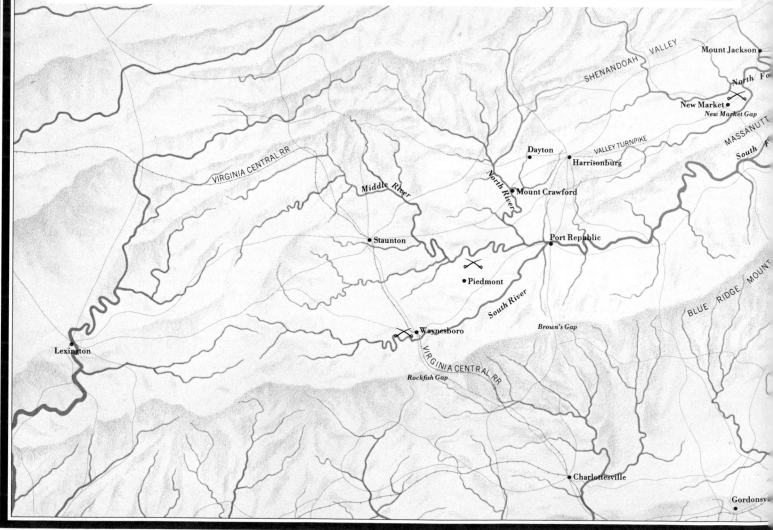

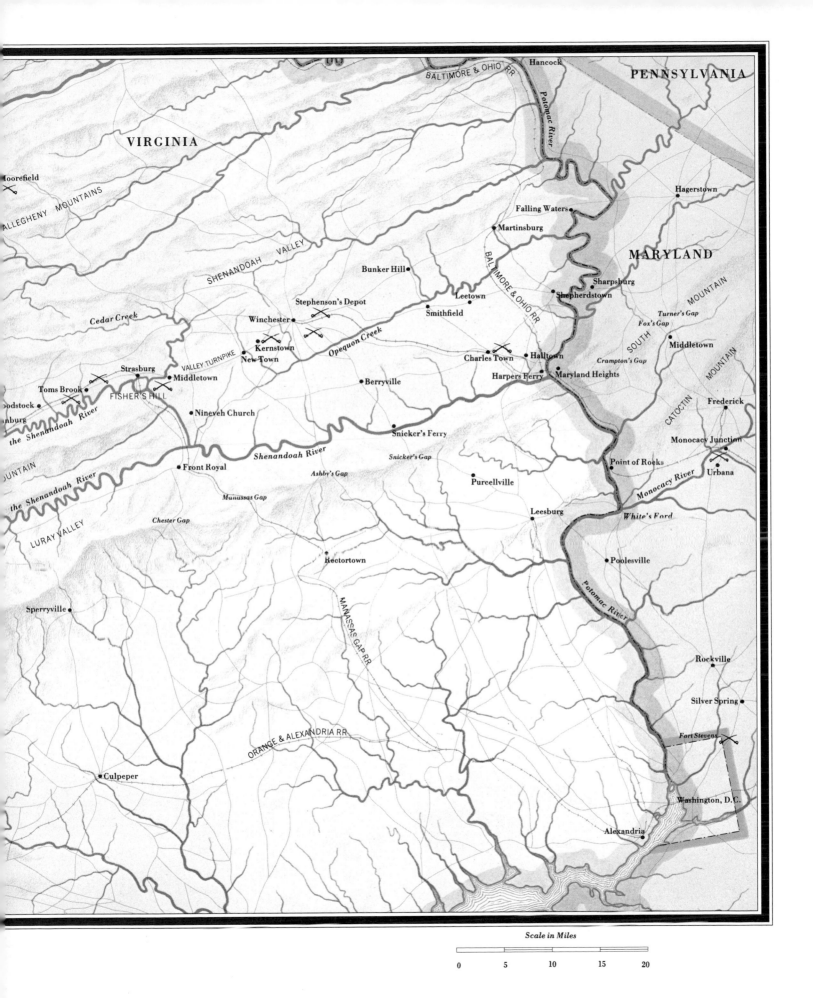

TIME
LIFE
BOOKS

This volume is one of a series that chronicles in full
the events of the American Civil War, 1861-1865.

The Cover: Major General Philip H. Sheridan gallops
past a line of cheering Union soldiers in this heroic
rendition of his storied, 20-mile ride from Winchester,
Virginia, to the battlefield at Cedar Creek on October 19, 1864. Sheridan's dramatic appearance infused
his army with renewed spirit, turning a Federal retreat
into a victory that ended Confederate dominion in the
Shenandoah Valley.

For information on and a full description of any of the
Time-Life Books series listed on this page, please call
1-800-621-7026 or write:
Reader Information
Time-Life Customer Service
P.O. Box C-32068
Richmond, Virginia 23261-2068

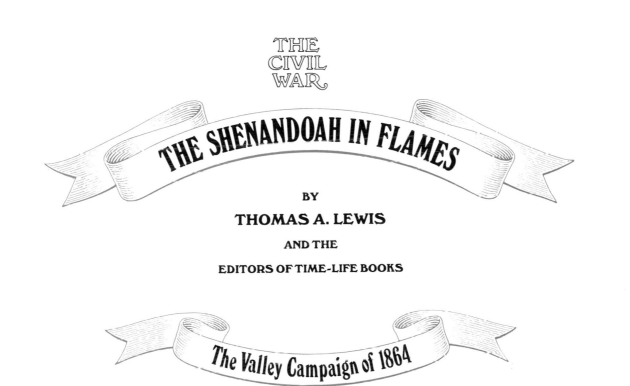

THE CIVIL WAR

THE SHENANDOAH IN FLAMES

BY

THOMAS A. LEWIS

AND THE

EDITORS OF TIME-LIFE BOOKS

The Valley Campaign of 1864

TIME-LIFE BOOKS, ALEXANDRIA, VIRGINIA

TIME-LIFE BOOKS

EDITOR-IN-CHIEF: Thomas H. Flaherty

Director of Editorial Resources: Elise D. Ritter-Clough
Executive Art Director: Ellen Robling
Director of Photography and Research:
John Conrad Weiser
Editorial Board: Dale M. Brown, Janet Cave, Roberta
Conlan, Robert Doyle, Laura Foreman, Jim Hicks,
Rita Thievon Mullin, Henry Woodhead
Assistant Director of Editorial Resources: Norma E. Shaw

PRESIDENT: John D. Hall

Vice President and Director of Marketing:
Nancy K. Jones
Editorial Director: Russell B. Adams, Jr.
Director of Production Services: Robert N. Carr
Production Manager: Prudence G. Harris
Supervisor of Quality Control: James King

Editorial Operations
Production: Celia Beattie
Library: Louise D. Forstall
Computer Composition: Deborah G. Tait (Manager),
Monika D. Thayer, Janet Barnes Syring,
Lillian Daniels
Interactive Media Specialist: Patti H. Cass

Time-Life Books is a division of Time Life
Incorporated

PRESIDENT AND CEO: John M. Fahey, Jr.

The Civil War

Series Director: Thomas H. Flaherty
Designer: Edward Frank
Series Administrator: Jane Edwin

Editorial Staff for *The Shenandoah in Flames*
Associate Editors: John Newton, David S. Thomson
(text); Jane N. Coughran (pictures)
Staff Writers: Margery duMond, Stephen G. Hyslop,
Daniel Stashower
Researchers: Trudy Pearson, Brian Pohanka (principals);
Harris Andrews
Assistant Designer: Lorraine D. Rivard
Copy Coordinator: Jayne E. Rohrich
Picture Coordinator: Betty H. Weatherley
Editorial Assistant: Donna Fountain
Special Contributor: Elissa E. Baldwin

Correspondents: Elisabeth Kraemer-Singh (Bonn);
Maria Vincenza Aloisi (Paris); Ann Natanson (Rome).
Valuable assistance was also provided by Judy Aspinall
(London); Christina Lieberman (New York).

The Author:
Thomas A. Lewis has been prowling the battlefields of the
Shenandoah Valley, his adopted home, for almost 20
years. His career as a journalist, writer and editor includes
a five-year stint as an editor for Time-Life Books and a
prior three-year tour as editor of the *Shenandoah Valley*
weekly newspaper in New Market, scene of the battle
described in chapter one.

The Consultants:
Colonel John R. Elting, USA (Ret.), a former Associate
Professor at West Point, is the author of *Battles for Scandi-
navia* in the Time-Life Books World War II series and of
*The Battle of Bunker's Hill, The Battles of Saratoga, Mili-
tary History and Atlas of the Napoleonic Wars, American
Army Life* and *The Superstrategists.* Co-author of *A Dictionary of Soldier Talk,* he is also editor of the three vol-
umes of *Military Uniforms in America, 1755-1867,* and associate editor of *The West Point Atlas of American Wars.*

William A. Frassanito, a Civil War historian and lecturer
specializing in photograph analysis, is the author of two
award-winning studies, *Gettysburg: A Journey in Time* and
*Antietam: The Photographic Legacy of America's Bloodiest
Day,* and a companion volume, *Grant and Lee, The Virginia Campaigns.* He has also served as chief consultant to the
photographic history series *The Image of War.*

Les Jensen, Director of the Second Armored Division
Museum, Fort Hood, Texas, specializes in Civil War arti-
facts and is a conservator of historic flags. He is a contributor to *The Image of War* series, consultant for numerous
Civil War publications and museums, and a member of
the Company of Military Historians. He was formerly Curator of the U.S. Army Transportation Museum at Fort
Eustis, Virginia, and before that Curator of the Museum
of the Confederacy in Richmond, Virginia.

Michael McAfee specializes in military uniforms and has
been Curator of Uniforms and History at the West Point
Museum since 1970. A fellow of the Company of Military
Historians, he coedited with Colonel Elting *Long Endure:
The Civil War Years,* and he collaborated with Frederick
Todd on *American Military Equipage.* He is the author of
Artillery of the American Revolution, 1775-1783, and has
written numerous articles for *Military Images Magazine.*

James P. Shenton, Professor of History at Columbia University, is a specialist in 19th-century American political
and social history, with particular emphasis on the Civil
War period. He is the author of *Robert John Walker* and
Reconstruction South.

Library of Congress Cataloguing in Publication Data
Lewis, Thomas A. 1942-
  The Shenandoah in flames.
  (The Civil War)
  Bibliography: p.
  Includes index.
  1. Shenandoah Valley Campaign, 1864 (May-
August)   I. Time-Life Books.   II. Title.
III. Series.
E476.66.L49 1987   973.7'37   86-14584
ISBN 0-8094-4784-3
ISBN 0-8094-4785-1 (lib. bdg.)

CONTENTS

The Valley Imperiled 16

"Black Dave's" Orgy of Fire 40

To the Gates of Washington 68

"I Want Sheridan" 100

Showdown at Cedar Creek 134

VMI's castle-like Barracks (*above*), built in 1851, was home to hundreds of young men who would become Confederate officers. The mood of the campus as war approached was made clear on Washington's Birthday in 1861 when cadets turned out to fire the traditional 13-gun salute: Flying from one of the flagpoles in place of the Stars and Stripes was a banner bearing a hand-lettered tribute to the cradle of secession — "Hurrah for South Carolina."

A view of the placid Shenandoah Valley town of Lexington in 1857 takes in the Barracks at VMI (*far right*) and the adjacent campus of Washington College (*center*), to which the name of Robert E. Lee would be joined after the War. Cadet John Wise remarked that there was little in Lexington to distract his classmates from their regimen: "The boy who finds allurement to idleness and vice in that town would discover it anywhere."

The Confederacy's Cradle for Command

For 17-year-old John S. Wise and other cadets at the Virginia Military Institute, the early months of 1864 were full of feverish anticipation. Though their tranquil campus in the Shenandoah Valley had not been disturbed by the enemy, a Confederate cavalry brigade was camped nearby — and visits from those cocky veterans goaded the student corps. "They jangled their spurs through the archway," Wise recalled, "and rode off as if they carried the world in a sling."

The fact that the restless cadets were held in reserve was a tribute to their institute. Scarcely 25 years old, VMI was such a valued source of officers that Confederate leaders were loath to risk losing its cadets in combat; their primary contribution had been to drill green troops at Richmond. One 33-year-old recruit later reflected on his boyish VMI instructor: "How I hated that little cadet! He was always so wide-awake, so clean, so interested in the drill."

As spring came in 1864, however, the cadets' season of innocence was about to end. A threat to the north would cause the youngsters Jefferson Davis once termed the "seed-corn of the Confederacy" to be cast into the fray.

A Founding Steeped in Martial Arts

Founded in 1839 at the state arsenal in Lexington (*below*), VMI bore the stamp of three resolute figures: Claudius Crozet (*far left*), a French engineer who had fought for Napoleon and who, as head of VMI's board, placed scientific training on a par with tactics; Captain John Preston (*center*), a shrewd lawyer who won state backing for the institute and taught there; and Major Francis H. Smith, a West Pointer who brought the rigorous tone of his alma mater to VMI as its first superintendent.

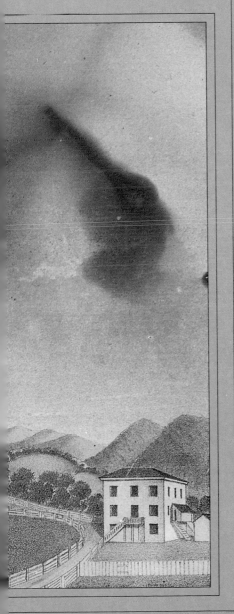

Matriculation Register of Cadets

No.	DATE OF ADMISSION	NAME	AGE	COUNTY OR TOWN	STATE
1	Nov. 11th 1839	John S. L. Logan	16	Rockbridge	Virginia
2	" " "	Philip J. Winn	19	Fluvanna	"
3	" " "	Thos. B. Cramer	22	Frederick	"
4	" " "	James Kenney	17	Rockingham	"
5	" " "	John W. Jones	16	Shenandoah	"
6	" " "	John J. Smith	16	Norfolk	"
7	" " "	James H. Jamison	19	Culpeper	"
8	" " "	Chas. F. Doyle	18	Roanoke	"
9	" " "	Valentine C. Saunders	18	Loudoun	"
10	" " "	W. M. Elliott	16	Buckingham	"
11	" " "	John O. Strange	16	Albemarle	"
12	" " "	Benj. Sharp	20	Lee	"
13	" " "	Chas. A. Cramp	17	Powhatan	"
14	" " "	O. M. Knight	16	Nottoway	"
15	" " "	B. B. Sills	18	Monongalia	"
16	" " "	Jas. S. Laurence	17	Caroline	"
17	" " "	Wm. Forbes	16	Richmond City	"
18	" " "	Henry B. Sumpter	17		"
19	" " "	Edmund Pendleton	16		"
20	" " "	Wm. L. Fair	17		"
21	" " "	Thos. B. Beale	16		"
22	" " "	Jos. M. Bell	20		"
23	" " "	C. E. Carter	18		"
24	" " "	Wm. S. Henderson	16		"
25	" " "	Louis A. Garnett	17		"
26	" " "	Jno. Marshall	16		"
27	" " "	Saml. B. Pryor	19		"
28	" " "	David Chilton	16		"
29	Dec 5 "	Jno. Lely Shields	18		"
30	" "	John E. Swann	17		"
31	March 1, /40	R. B. Washington	17		"
32	July 20 "	Ben. Estill	20		"
33	" "	Edmund Winston	18		"
34	" " "	James L. Bryan	16		"
35	" " "	James J. Preston	16		"
36	" " "	J. B. Dorman	16		"
37	" " "	And. J. Hamilton	17		"
38	" " "	Jno. Sharp	20		"
39	" " "	Elisha F. Paxton	17		"
40	" " "	Wm. J. Warden	16		"
41	" " "	R. C. W. Radford	17		"
42	" " "	G. W. Kinney	17		"
43	" " "	John L. Peyton	16		"

As this register shows, a majority of the cadets in VMI's inaugural class — all Virginians — were under 18. The first of 20 candidates to win admission in 1839 with full financial support from the state was William A. Forbes of Richmond (*above*). Like many of VMI's early graduates, Forbes became a teacher but returned to uniform during the Civil War as colonel of the 14th Tennessee; he was mortally wounded at Second Bull Run.

Lessons from an Unsung Professor

Major Thomas Jonathan Jackson (*left*) joined the VMI faculty in 1851 to teach science and artillery tactics — a career he was still pursuing six years later when this picture was taken. Though destined for greatness, Jackson inspired little awe among the cadets. He once reported a youngster who lagged while hauling a cannon for "not trotting" at drill; the accused responded, "I am a natural pacer."

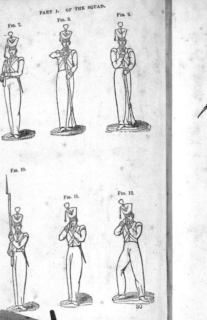

Steeped in such texts as this manual prepared by Samuel Cooper — later adjutant general of the Confederate Army — the young Lexington cadets became masters of the drill. A reporter who observed them on parade remarked: "I do not think older persons could be taught the exercise as they are."

Cadets learned the mysteries of such instruments as the condenser and the telegraph (*left*). When Jackson's technical courses proved baffling, the institute built him a laboratory in the hope that "the experimental illustrations will hereafter be made more full and complete."

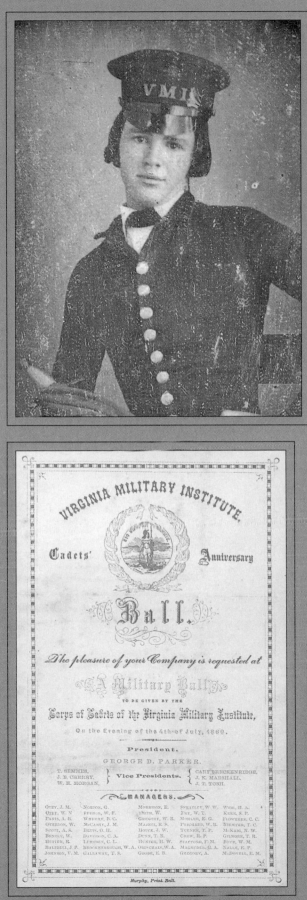

At left, an unidentified youth wears a cadet's furlough coat. For ceremonial occasions, the corps turned out in the West Point-inspired full-dress uniform worn by Daniel Lee Powell (*below*), captain of cadets in 1847. During the Civil War, Powell served as lieutenant colonel of the 19th Virginia Militia.

At right, roommates do their best to amuse themselves in a scene sketched by a cadet in 1855. For a corps allowed few indulgences — one rule stipulated "No cadet shall be allowed to keep a waiter, horse or dog" — the annual Fourth of July ball was a rare treat. Reflecting the times, the invitation to the 1860 gala (*left*) defiantly bore the seal of Virginia; earlier invitations had featured a bald eagle and the motto: *E Pluribus Unum.*

Cadets Yearning for Battle

Lieutenant Colonel Scott Shipp (*above*), an 1859 VMI graduate, was cadet commandant in May 1864 when his students were called on to help counter a fresh Federal thrust into the Shenandoah Valley; 17 of those he led from Lexington are shown here with their cadet ranks. Others may have sensed that the tide of war was running against the South, but John Wise, who marched with the corps, noted, "Here, in this little band of fledglings, the hope of battle flamed as brightly as on the morning of Manassas."

CORPORAL
HARDAWAY
DINWIDDIE

PRIVATE
GAYLORD
CLARK

PRIVATE EDWARD TUTWILER

CORPORAL
THOMAS HAYES

PRIVATE RICHARD TUNSTALL

PRIVATE JOHN WEBB   PRIVATE ROBERT COUSINS   CORPORAL PATRICK HENRY   PRIVATE NICHOLAS BAYARD   PRIVATE FLEMING JAMES

CAPTAIN BENJAMIN COLONNA

SERGEANT WILLIAM NELSON

PRIVATE MOSES EZEKIEL

CORPORAL JOHN JAMES   **PRIVATE JOHN CRICHTON**   **CORPORAL GEORGE MACON**   **PRIVATE HUGH FRY**

The Valley Imperiled

"We drank in greedily the praise which made us the lions of the hour."

CORPORAL JOHN S. WISE, VIRGINIA MILITARY INSTITUTE CADET, AFTER THE BATTLE OF NEW MARKET, MAY 15, 1864

1

On the evening of May 10, 1864, a couple of hours after dark, a messenger on a lathered horse galloped up to the fortress-like main building of the Virginia Military Institute at Lexington, Virginia. That day the cadets had enjoyed a respite from their usual round of duties and classes. It was the first anniversary of the death of Lieutenant General Thomas Jonathan (Stonewall) Jackson, a former VMI professor, and the boys' only activities had been a morning memorial ceremony and an evening parade. They had gone to bed at 9 p.m., but many of them were sufficiently awake to wonder about the sudden pounding of hoofs and the hasty gathering of officers by lantern light near the institute's statue of George Washington.

Moments later the drums rattled the long roll, calling the young men to an emergency assembly on the parade ground. Such a commotion usually meant that a cadet was absent without leave or that there was a fire in town; it did not occur to the students that this drum roll had anything to do with the War. However ardently these young men had followed every detail of the fighting and had yearned to be a part of it, rarely in three years had any serious alarm filtered through to these tranquil, manicured grounds.

But after the startled cadets had tumbled into formation, they heard their adjutant read an electrifying message: Major General John C. Breckinridge, commander of the Confederate Department of Western Virginia, urgently required their services. They were to march at dawn for his headquarters at Staunton, 32 miles to the northeast. The VMI cadets were going to war.

"The air was rent with wild cheering," wrote cadet Corporal John S. Wise, "at the thought that our hour was come at last." After working all night to assemble their gear, pack the wagons and load the caissons, more than 200 cadets formed up on the parade ground at first light. At the order from their amiable, overweight commandant of cadets, Lieutenant Colonel Scott Shipp, they playfully stomped across the rickety little bridge leading from the campus, making the span sway and groan, and marched jauntily northward down the valley of the Shenandoah.

The expedition of the exuberant boy soldiers was a poignant illustration of the Confederacy's increasingly desperate straits. This was no ordinary militia unit; this was the student body of the West Point of the South, the school that had provided 425 of the thousand or so trained army officers available to the Confederacy when the Civil War began. These young men, ranging in age from 15 to 25 years, were to be the next generation of military leaders. Their intelligence, training, spirit and, above all, their promise were quite simply irreplaceable. Any threat that could justify using them in combat had to be a deadly one indeed.

The threat was real enough. General Robert E. Lee's outnumbered and malnourished Army of Northern Virginia was being forced to retreat southward through the forests of the Wilderness toward Spotsylvania Court

This Austrian-made rifle was knocked from the grasp of VMI cadet Charles Henry Read by Federal shellfire as the cadet corps went into action at New Market, Virginia, on May 15, 1864. Though the blast mangled his weapon beyond repair, Read escaped with only a minor wound.

House — and Richmond — by the Army of the Potomac. Pressed as never before, Lee not only had to fend off the Federals — who had been energized by their grim new chief, Lieutenant General Ulysses S. Grant — but also had to feed his men.

For relief, Lee looked as always to the Shenandoah. This lush strip of fertile, riverbottom land along Virginia's western border was the breadbasket of the South. Unlike the war-blasted terrain of eastern Virginia, the Valley, protected by the barrier of the Blue Ridge Mountains, had not been trampled by large armies. There had been battles, of course, during Stonewall Jackson's Valley Campaign of 1862. Lee had used the Shenandoah as an invasion route to Maryland in 1862 and Pennsylvania in 1863. But the fighting had been relatively small in scale and infrequent. Between engagements, the hard-working people and their productive farms had been little disturbed.

The Shenandoah is but one section of a long valley that runs from southwest Virginia to Pennsylvania. The southernmost springs that nurture the Shenandoah River rise near Lexington, run generally northward past Staunton and coalesce into the South Fork of the Shenandoah near Port Republic, 20 miles farther northeast.

Here the river is confronted by Massanutten Mountain, a 45-mile-long cluster of ridges that cleaves the Valley floor from Harrisonburg and Port Republic in the south to Front Royal and Strasburg in the north.

The river's North Fork rises in the Alleghenies and meanders eastward to New Market, about halfway along the Massanutten, then northward along the mountain's western flank. The North Fork valley is considered the Shenandoah; the area of the South

Fork across the Massanutten is called the Luray, or Page, Valley. The two tributaries meet at Front Royal; after traversing the broadest section of the Valley, the Shenandoah joins the Potomac River 130 miles northeast of Lexington, amid the splendid, riven cliffs of Harpers Ferry.

Despite repeated Federal incursions, the Confederates had held onto the Valley for three years. Now more than ever Lee could not afford to lose it. The hungry Confederacy desperately needed the calves fattening on its sweet grass; the flour that its mills would grind in a month or two when the winter wheat had ripened; the autumn crops of corn and fruit; and the poultry, milk, vegetables, eggs and butter that flowed from this quiet cornucopia.

Federal occupation would also mean the loss of the Virginia Central Railroad, with its major station at Staunton. It would put within enemy reach the Virginia & Tennessee Railroad, which snaked its way to Richmond through the eastern foothills of the Blue Ridge Mountains. Perhaps even worse, a Federal force in the Valley would be behind Lee's left flank. A sudden assault from that direction could prove fatal to the Army of Northern Virginia.

There were few Confederate forces to counter these dark possibilities. Brigadier General John D. Imboden, at his Valley District headquarters in Staunton, had only 1,600 cavalrymen to guard this portion of the Valley. The nearest help was 155 miles away at Dublin, in southwestern Virginia, where Breckinridge was stationed with 6,500 men.

When Lee learned early in May that two Federal armies were threatening the Valley — one from the west, by way of Dublin, another from the northern, or lower, end of

Major General John C. Breckinridge, commander of the Confederate Department of Western Virginia in 1864, was vilified in the North for turning against the Union he had served as Vice President before the War. In December 1863 the New York *Times* greeted with open delight a rumor that Breckinridge had been killed in action: "If it be true that a loyal bullet has sent this traitor to eternity, every loyal heart feels satisfaction and will not scruple to express it."

the Valley at Martinsburg — he asked Richmond to attach Imboden's and Breckinridge's forces to his command so that he could more efficiently protect his vital lines of supply and communication.

In the impending conflict, the armies would be returning to fight on old battlefields near Winchester, Cedar Creek and Port Republic, and to consecrate new ones at New Market, Piedmont and Fisher's Hill. The Valley Campaign of 1864 would not be confined to the Shenandoah. It would begin in the remote valleys of the Alleghenies to the west and along the banks of the New River far to the south; it would reach Lynchburg in June and spread to the outskirts of Washington, D.C., in July.

The fighting would be distinguished by heroism and brilliant generalship, and it would be marred by blundering and stupidity. But it would be remembered above all for what the local people would call "the Burning." This campaign of systematic destruction by Union troops, provoked by the frustrations of a war gone on too long, would be unleashed against civilians and their private property on a scale not seen in America since the Revolution. Soon, many residents of the bountiful Shenandoah would experience an unfamiliar sensation — hunger.

John Cabell Breckinridge of Kentucky had decided young that the law would be his profession but politics would be his life. His determination and abilities were such that he had risen to heights few men achieve. In 1856, at the age of 35, he had become the youngest man ever elected Vice President of the United States; in 1859, near the end of his term, the Kentucky legislature elected him to the U.S. Senate. The next year, the Southern wing of the fractured Democratic Party nominated him for President. Although an unwilling candidate — he knew the split in his party assured the election of the Republican Abraham Lincoln — Breckinridge ran a respectable race, garnering 18 percent of the popular vote and finishing second, ahead of Stephen A. Douglas and John Bell in the electoral vote.

But Breckinridge's fortunes changed as he continued to fight for moderation in an increasingly partisan time. Returning to the Senate after the Republican victory, he argued at first in favor of Constitutional guarantees for slavery in order to prevent secession; then he condemned as unconstitutional the harsh measures taken by the Lincoln Administration as the War began — such as imprisonment without trial and unlawful searches and seizures. Those proposing to fight a war to preserve the Constitution, he insisted, must uphold it themselves.

In the poisonous atmosphere of 1861, such reasoned stances won him no friends and Breckinridge soon left the Senate. Shortly thereafter, Kentucky, despite his passionate opposition, abandoned neutrality and took up the Union cause. After some hesitation, Breckinridge joined the Confederate Army; he was declared a traitor by the U.S. Senate and was sought for arrest. Forced to choose between imprisonment and armed resistance, the former Vice President said he preferred "the musket of a soldier."

Although Breckinridge had tried to prevent war, he learned to wage it well. Commissioned a brigadier general, he led his men competently at Shiloh, Corinth and Vicksburg. But he had the misfortune to serve under one of the Confederacy's most egocentric generals, Braxton Bragg, who frequently blamed his defeats on his subordinates. After bungling the Battle of Chattanooga in November 1863, Bragg censured Breckinridge for poor performance.

Thus by the age of 43, Breckinridge was branded in the North as a traitor and in the South as the man responsible for losing Chattanooga. But few who knew him accepted either judgment. Confederate General John B. Gordon, who met Breckinridge in Tennessee and would serve under him in the Valley, was unreserved in his admiration. "Tall, erect, and commanding in physique," Gordon wrote later, "he would have been selected in any martial group as a typical leader. Under fire and in extreme peril he was strikingly courageous, alert and self-poised." When the Confederacy needed a strong general to lead the atrophied forces in the Department of Western Virginia early in 1864, Breckinridge was a logical choice.

The department assigned to Breckinridge was enormous; it included southwestern Virginia, a portion of eastern Tennessee, and any parts of Kentucky and West Virginia that the Confederates could take and hold. In addition to the Virginia & Tennessee Railroad, it contained two industries of great strategic importance: the salt works at Saltville, from which came a large percentage of the preservative for the Confederate Army's meat rations, and the lead mines of Wytheville, source of precious bullets.

To protect all this, Breckinridge found in his department a few brigades of poorly disciplined infantry, some dismounted cavalrymen, and a few cannon, most of them out of commission. Breckinridge assumed command on the 4th of March, and after six weeks of furious work he had assembled a respectable little army.

It was none too soon. On May 2, Brigadier General George Crook marched out of the Kanawha Valley in West Virginia with 6,000 Federal infantrymen, heading southeast toward Dublin. His mission was to sever the Virginia & Tennessee Railroad at the New River Bridge while his 2,000 cavalrymen, under Brigadier General William W. Averell, rode a more southerly circuit to strike Saltville and Wytheville. Then the whole force was to move north to Staunton and cut the Virginia Central.

Breckinridge was preparing to fend off Crook when his brigades were incorporated into Robert E. Lee's Army of Northern Virginia. Breckinridge soon received urgent orders from Lee to confront a second Federal army of 9,000 men under Major General Franz Sigel that was marching south into the Shenandoah from Martinsburg. "Grant's whole army is moving on our right," Lee told Breckinridge on May 4, the eve of the Battle of the Wilderness. Sigel's army from Martinsburg, he added, "will probably cross at Chester Gap and move upon our left."

Breckinridge responded swiftly. He ordered his two largest infantry brigades — slightly more than half his army — to march from Dublin to Staunton, 155 miles away. Urged on by the embattled Lee, Breckinridge and his staff covered the distance on horseback in just three days, arriving on May 8. The two infantry brigades lagged well in the rear although Brigadier Generals John Echols — despite a weak heart that would repeatedly disable him — and Gabriel Wharton drove the men to the brink of exhaustion in a series of forced marches.

Meanwhile, the troops Breckinridge left behind, perhaps 4,000 men in all, scrambled to meet the rapidly approaching infantry of

Brigadier General George Crook, who led the Federal assault on the Virginia & Tennessee Railroad, was experienced in the unconventional warfare necessitated by the rough terrain of southwestern Virginia. Before the War, Crook had fought Indians in Oregon, and he carried until his death in 1890 a reminder of that campaign — an arrowhead lodged deep in his hip.

Brigadier General William Averell, whose troopers made feints while Crook's infantry suffered losses, was a commander of some daring. He seemed tentative, however, when operating as part of a larger force. A year earlier at Chancellorsville, the volatile Joseph Hooker had relieved him of duty with a stinging indictment: "I could excuse General Averell if I could anywhere discover in his operations a desire to find and engage the enemy."

George Crook and Averell's Federal cavalry. Facing two foes, the Confederates split up. A brigade of infantry and one of cavalry remained at Dublin while two understrength cavalry brigades guarded the passes between Saltville and the Narrows of the New River.

The Confederate cavalrymen guarding the Saltville passes were soon handed what amounted to a minor victory. As Averell and his Federal troopers were heading for the salt works, they heard a rumor that the formidable John Hunt Morgan and his feared Confederate raiders were dead ahead. Averell therefore contented himself with a feint toward Saltville and its few defenders on May 8 and shied off to seek easier going at Wytheville — where ironically he did run into Morgan and was soundly beaten.

The 3,000 Confederates defending Dublin did not get off as easily as their comrades holding the passes. The commander at Dublin, Brigadier General Albert Jenkins, had entrenched his men a few miles north of town on the crest of a steep hill named Cloyd's Mountain, across the road leading to the vital New River railroad bridge. It was a good position and looked far stronger than it actually was.

But George Crook, made of sterner stuff than Averell, was not daunted. "They may whip us," he is reported to have growled, "but I guess not." Whereupon he ordered one of his brigades to work its way through thick woods around the Confederate right flank and attack. Then the rest of the Federal force, including a brigade commanded by a future U.S. President, Colonel Rutherford B. Hayes, charged the Confederate center.

At the foot of Cloyd's Mountain, Hayes's men encountered a stream. Although small, its steep banks and waist-deep water made it

At left, Colonel Rutherford B. Hayes (*center*) of the 23rd Ohio presides over a mock duel early in the War. The future President saw fighting in earnest when he led a brigade against Confederates blocking the way to the New River Bridge on May 9, 1864. As illustrated below by a witness, Hayes's Federals (*foreground*) faced deadly fire as they prepared to ford a stream below Cloyd's Mountain and assault the enemy on the slope.

difficult to cross, and Hayes ordered a halt at the bottom of the ridge to restore his formation. The respite was particularly appreciated by one officer whose high cavalry boots had filled with water, nearly immobilizing him. The men who went to the officer's assistance were shocked to recognize General Crook himself, who had been charging in the middle of the front line. It was a rare thing for a general to do, and a lieutenant in the 23rd Ohio later remarked that the only problem with a general leading a charge was that he had to be helped.

Meanwhile, the flank attack had failed to dislodge the Confederates. "I could distinctly see a sheet of flames issuing from the rebel works," Colonel Daniel D. Johnson of the 14th West Virginia reported later, "but could not see a single rebel." The Federals pulled themselves together, charged again and succeeded in driving the outnumbered defenders from their line.

In the ensuing melee, the Confederates lost more than 530 men, among them General Jenkins, who was mortally wounded. Colonel John McCausland took command of the shaken men as they made a fighting withdrawal through Dublin and retreated eight miles farther east to the New River Bridge. "I found the works at this place incomplete and untenable," McCausland reported later; instead of making a stand in front of the bridge, he crossed to the far side.

The Federals, who had suffered nearly 700 casualties in the 90-minute fight, halted for the night in Dublin. Not until the next morning did they approach the massive, 400-foot wooden bridge they had come to destroy. McCausland tried to keep them away from the span with artillery fire from across the river, which the Federals returned. Crook allowed the gunners a two-hour duel, then ordered a party onto the bridge to set it afire. As the flames consumed the impressive structure, the men on both sides ceased firing and lined the banks to watch — while a Federal band played martial airs.

Then, with his first mission accomplished, Crook suffered a curious failure of resolve. Instead of joining Sigel in order to advance on Lynchburg as Grant wanted, he retreated into the Alleghenies. Crook explained later that he had seen a captured dispatch claiming a Confederate victory over Grant in the Wilderness and that he feared being cut off by forces detached from Lee's army. Crook's timidity would prove costly, for it would allow Breckinridge to fight on a single front.

Soon joined by Averell, who had been

driven back from Wytheville, Crook and his weary army set out in pouring rain on a grueling, 50-mile withdrawal. Nine days later they went into bivouac in Meadow Bluff, West Virginia, for the time being out of the campaign they had so forcefully begun.

While Breckinridge raced north to meet Sigel, that Federal commander was moving sluggishly southward—but not to attempt the flanking movement feared by Lee. Grant did not have enough confidence in Sigel to have given him such a difficult assignment.

German-born Franz Sigel was a prime example of the Civil War generals who attained high rank without having demonstrated their military competence. When the War began, Sigel had been superintendent of schools and a leader of the large German community in St. Louis, Missouri. He received a commission, and rapid promotion to major general, primarily to encourage enlistment among the 1.25 million German-Americans living in the North. His high visibility without doubt spurred thousands of these Germans to volunteer.

But his qualifications to be a commander were dubious at best. He claimed to have led troops in three battles during the German revolts of the 1840s. He failed to mention that he had been resoundingly defeated each time. Worse, he used his high standing among German-Americans to pressure the government, urging his fellow immigrants to regard any setback to his career as an insult to their nationality. After the Federal defeat at Fredericksburg, for example, Sigel had been put temporarily in command of one of the grand divisions of the reorganized Army of the Potomac. When he was returned to his own corps, which unhappily for him was not

Major General Franz Sigel, in command of Federal operations in the Shenandoah Valley, enjoyed a devoted following among his fellow German immigrants, whose loyalty to their natty general inspired a comic wartime ballad (*opposite*). Soldiers in the Valley grew disenchanted with his leadership, however, and gave the song a new refrain: "I fights no more mit Sigel."

the largest, he demanded to be relieved. For a year he stumped the country raising a great German uproar over his misfortune. At length President Lincoln gave him command of the Department of West Virginia, largely to shut him up.

The political nature of the assignment disgusted Colonel David Hunter Strother, who was a staff officer under Sigel's command. "The Dutch vote must be secured at all hazards," Strother wrote sarcastically in his diary. "And the sacrifice of West Virginia is a small matter."

As badly as Grant wanted action in the Valley, he expected little of his self-serving department commander. It was Crook, Grant thought, who although subordinate to Sigel would do the important work; Grant even

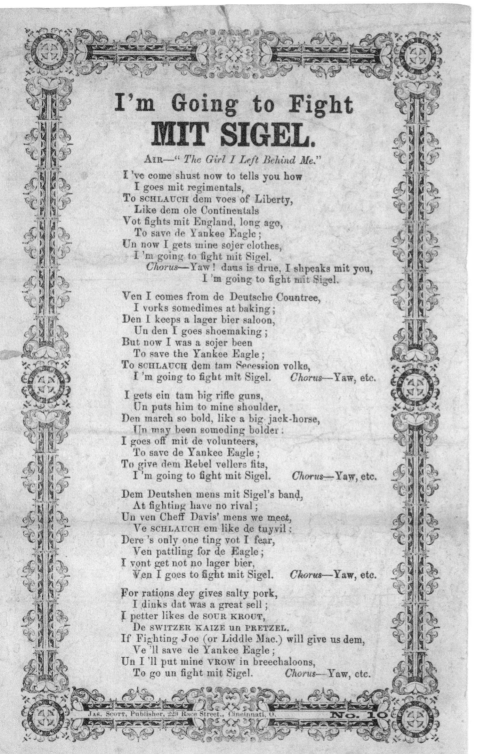

I'm Going to Fight MIT SIGEL.

AIR—"*The Girl I Left Behind Me.*"

I've come shust now to tells you how
    I goes mit regimentals,
To SCHLAUCH dem voes of Liberty,
    Like dem ole Continentals
Vot fights mit England, long ago,
    To save de Yankee Eagle;
Un now I gets mine sojer clothes,
    I'm going to fight mit Sigel.
        Chorus—Yaw! daus is drue, I shpeaks mit you,
            I'm going to fight mit Sigel.

Ven I comes from de Deutsche Countree,
    I vorks somedimes at baking;
Den I keeps a lager bier saloon,
    Un den I goes shoemaking;
But now I was a sojer been
    To save the Yankee Eagle;
To SCHLAUCH dem tam Secession volks,
    I'm going to fight mit Sigel.   *Chorus*—Yaw, etc.

I gets ein tam big rifle guns,
    Un puts him to mine shoulder,
Den march so bold, like a big jack-horse,
    Un may been someding bolder:
I goes off mit de volunteers,
    To save de Yankee Eagle;
To give dem Rebel vellers fits,
    I'm going to fight mit Sigel.   *Chorus*—Yaw, etc.

Dem Deutshen mens mit Sigel's band,
    At fighting have no rival;
Un ven Cheff Davis' mens we meet,
    Ve SCHLAUCH em like de tuyvil:
Dere's only one ting vot I fear,
    Ven pattling for de Eagle;
I vont get not no lager bier,
    Ven I goes to fight mit Sigel.   *Chorus*—Yaw, etc.

For rations dey gives salty pork,
    I dinks dat was a great sell;
I petter likes de SOUR KROUT,
    De SWITZER KAIZE un PRETZEL.
If Fighting Joe (or Liddle Mac.) will give us dem,
    Ve'll save de Yankee Eagle;
Un I'll put mine VROW in breechaloons,
    To go un fight mit Sigel.   *Chorus*—Yaw, etc.

JAS. SCOTT, Publisher, 229 Race Street, Cincinnati, O.   NO. 10

summoned Crook to a personal briefing in Culpeper, Virginia, to make sure his instructions would not be mishandled by Sigel.

All Sigel would have to do, in Grant's view, was guard the northern portion of the Valley and the Baltimore & Ohio Railroad, which ran along the Potomac. Then, as an afterthought, Grant decided that any army was better off on the march than in camp. Sigel could at least meet Crook in Staunton with reinforcements and supplies. "If Sigel can't skin, himself," said Grant, borrowing a line from Abraham Lincoln, "he can hold a leg whilst someone else skins."

Thus on April 29, Sigel headed timidly up the Valley. Stopping frequently, flinging out patrols in every direction, he took three days to cover the 22 miles from Martinsburg to Winchester. Then, beset by rumors of enemy forces to his front and flanks and rear, he stopped again.

Sigel lingered in Winchester for days, whiling away the time by drilling his men. Perplexed officers tried to execute maneuvers they had never heard of while Sigel and his staff — many of them fellow immigrants — shouted orders at them in German.

Sigel demanded obedience. "I don't want any suggestions from Battalion Commanders!" he bellowed on one occasion. "All I want from them is to listen carefully to the orders, as they are issued, and to repeat them, precisely as they are received."

The confusion reached its zenith on May 5, when Sigel staged a mock battle. At the outset of the exercise, the 34th Massachusetts was ordered to move forward as a skirmish line. While infantry units behind them marched and countermarched, batteries galloped from position to position and cavalry charged this way and that, the men of the

34th tramped on, forgotten. They struggled "over fences, through swamps, across ravines and in woodland," Lieutenant Colonel William S. Lincoln recalled, in "strict obedience" to orders. At the end of the long day, he wrote, the army counted its casualties: "Killed, none; wounded, none; missing, the 34th Massachusetts Infantry." By the time frantic couriers found the still-advancing regiment and brought the men back to camp, darkness had fallen. The fiasco, said one Federal officer, "bred in everyone the most supreme contempt for General Sigel and his crowd of foreign adventurers."

While Sigel was preoccupied with drilling and sham battles, his logistics were falling into disarray. Supply trains dispatched from Martinsburg were plundered by partisan rangers — most effectively by the 43rd Virginia Cavalry Battalion under the legendary Lieutenant Colonel John S. Mosby, operating out of the Blue Ridge Mountains. After

the Confederates captured Sigel's personal supply train, he ordered each subsequent caravan guarded by 400 cavalrymen.

But the partisans who caused Sigel the deepest embarrassment were a company of rangers from General John Imboden's command. These horsemen were led by a Virginia cavalry captain named John H. (Hanse) McNeill, a young cavalier as dashing and courageous as Mosby.

On May 5, the day Sigel was staging his mock battle, McNeill and 60 men emerged from their West Virginia hideouts and destroyed a B & O repair shop and storage yard. Stung by rebukes from Washington at his failure to protect the railroad, Sigel sent 500 cavalrymen under Colonel Jacob Higgins in futile pursuit of the elusive McNeill.

By this time Sigel's every move was being reported, virtually within minutes, to Imboden at Woodstock by Confederate signalmen perched atop Shenandoah Peak, the

Broad and straight, the Valley Turnpike with its macadam surface was the main thoroughfare for Sigel's army as it pushed south in early May. Confronting the Federals along the strategic route were grim reminders of past battles. An aide to Sigel recalled: "Graves and dead animals in all stages of decomposition marked the way."

2,300-foot crest at the north end of Massanutten Mountain. Thus Imboden knew that a cavalry force had gone after McNeill; that Sigel had resumed his march south, only to stop again near Strasburg; and that another cavalry detachment — 500 men of Colonel William H. Boyd's 1st New York Cavalry — was headed east around Massanutten Mountain and up the Luray Valley toward New Market Gap.

Imboden was worried by the information. Breckinridge had arrived in Staunton on May 8, but he was far ahead of his infantry and at the moment had only a few hundred militiamen at his disposal. Besides, Staunton was more than 70 miles to the southwest of Sigel's position at Strasburg. Imboden himself had 1,600 cavalry. Sigel had

to be checked, but how was it to be done?

Imboden had an idea. Considering the Federal commander's performance to date, Imboden reckoned that Sigel would advance no farther until his wide-ranging cavalry patrols reassured him that the roads were clear. The best way to slow him, Imboden decided, was "to attack these detachments as far from Strasburg as possible and delay their return as long as possible."

Leaving only 500 troopers in front of Sigel's army, Imboden on May 9 took 800 men and rode to the northwest, into the Alleghenies. By dawn they had traversed 20 rugged miles of little-traveled mountain passes and had set up an ambush at Baker, West Virginia, on the Lost River.

Minutes after daybreak, Colonel Jacob

The north end of Massanutten Mountain, seen from Strasburg, gave Confederate signalmen a commanding view of Union movements, providing intelligence supplemented by reports from scouts and spies. But occasionally the flow of information was interrupted. An officer told Breckinridge on May 11 that frequent patrols had sealed off enemy lines and clouds were making "observation from the mountain impossible."

Higgins' Federal cavalry patrol, on its way back after failing to catch McNeill, trotted into view. Seeing a few Confederate riders fleeing into a narrow gap, Higgins ordered a charge — into the jaws of Imboden's trap. As hidden Confederates opened fire from the slopes on either side of the gap, the Federal troopers wheeled about and began what one of them called "a ride for life."

Imboden's riders thundered close behind the desperate Federals, who abandoned their wagons to speed their flight. Imboden gave Higgins' horsemen little rest until the Federals crossed the Potomac River into Maryland, 60 miles from the site of the ambush.

By nine that evening, Imboden was back in the Valley reporting his success to Breckinridge by telegraph from Mount Jackson, a town 24 miles south of Strasburg. He had left his troopers behind, "much jaded, and camped tonight on the head of Lost River. They will be here by 4 p.m. tomorrow." The question was whether they would be back in time, for despite the rout of Higgins' command, Sigel had started to move again. He reached Woodstock on May 11, and the next day sent a cavalry advance toward Mount Jackson. Imboden and his skeleton force fell back toward New Market, seven miles farther south, while keeping an eye out for Colonel Boyd's 1st New York Cavalry, which had been scouting somewhere on the eastern flank of Massanutten Mountain.

All day on May 13, Imboden kept his men in line of battle, determined to hold Sigel north of New Market. "By what hour," he asked Breckinridge tensely, "can I expect support here?" Late in the afternoon Imboden learned to his relief that Sigel had not yet left Woodstock with his infantry. Boyd was still a threat, but "if he comes on," Imboden

wired Breckinridge from New Market, "I will fight him here." Just as the telegraph operator finished keying that message, hundreds of Federal horsemen appeared in the gap above the town.

On the mountain, Boyd had come to the mistaken conclusion that the soldiers and wagons he could see in and around New Market were part of Sigel's command, although he thought it strange that the supply wagons were positioned ahead of the army. Ignoring the apparent oddity, Boyd led his column down toward the town.

As the unsuspecting Federals approached New Market, a boy named Elon Henkel heard a rumbling noise and ran to the front of his Main Street home to investigate. There he saw Imboden's two regiments pounding toward him "neck and neck, the horses' hoofs hammering the pike, the scabbards of the sabers rattling, and the cavalrymen giving the Rebel yell." While Henkel fled for cover, the Confederate horsemen turned at the crossroads and galloped toward Boyd's New Yorkers, who were nearing a bridge over Smith's Creek, east of town.

Shouting orders as he rode, Imboden sent the 23rd Virginia to engage the Federals at the bridge while he circled around them with the 18th Virginia and two guns. Boyd's men were crossing the creek when the 23rd Virginia hit them; the astonished Federals, outnumbered 2 to 1, tried to make a stand, but within moments they were virtually surrounded. They attempted to break out with a desperate charge to the rear, only to find that the road behind them was blocked by the 18th Virginia.

The Federals' only alternative was to retreat up the mountain slopes, into the cover

Weary Virginia troops converse amicably with a young woman in the gateway to her home in this painting by Confederate veteran William Sheppard. Although a number of the Shenandoah Valley's proverbially independent-minded citizens remained loyal to the Union, the majority bristled at the prospect of Federal occupation and offered what comfort they could to the Southerners defending their fertile soil.

ers ineffective. As for Boyd's men, "They are wandering in the mountain tonight cut off," Imboden told Breckinridge with grim satisfaction. "Colonel Boyd was wounded. We have his horse, and he is in the brush."

Breckinridge by this time had made a difficult decision. The loss of the New River Bridge to Crook had caused his old enemy, Braxton Bragg — now an adviser to President Jefferson Davis — to recommend that Breckinridge be ordered back to southwest Virginia to stop Crook. The decision was ultimately left to Robert E. Lee and Lee was not sure what was wise. On May 11, during a break in the heavy fighting near Spotsylvania Court House, he wired Breckinridge tersely: "You must judge."

As there was no sign of a further advance by Crook, Breckinridge decided to defend the Valley. His men expected him to stay put and fortify Staunton, to make up for his disadvantage in numbers. But Breckinridge's idea of defense was to attack. He would lead his 3,500 infantrymen and two batteries north toward Sigel and "give him battle wherever found."

Breckinridge ordered his men to move out at dawn on May 13, the VMI cadets arriving just in time to advance with them. Late on the 12th, ignoring their blistered feet and a heavy rainstorm, they had stepped snappily into Staunton while their fifers played "The Girl I Left behind Me." Breckinridge's veterans looked over the young faces and the natty gray uniforms — and welcomed the self-conscious cadets with a chorus of nursery rhymes.

Seventy miles away, General Sigel had decided it was too dangerous to go farther south than Woodstock. "If Breckinridge should advance against us," he told Washington

of the woods. "Our men were seen running in all directions on foot," wrote Captain James H. Stevenson of the 1st New York, "their horses having given out or got fast among the rocks; while some of the horses rushed along wildly, without riders, the saddles under their bellies."

In three days, the hard-riding Imboden had smashed two enemy forces that were 30 mountainous miles apart. He had caused roughly 150 casualties. More important, he had rendered more than 800 Federal troop-

bravely, "I will resist him at some convenient location." But on learning of Boyd's defeat, Sigel was seized by a sense of urgency. On May 14, he ordered Colonel Augustus Moor, commander of one of his two infantry brigades, to assemble a force of infantry, cavalry and artillery from various commands — 2,350 men in all, approximately one third of Sigel's army — and make a reconnaissance.

The order troubled Moor. Only one of his three regiments — the 123rd Ohio — was from his own brigade, the others coming from Colonel Joseph Thoburn's brigade. "I asked for scouts, or a reliable map of the Valley, as I had no knowledge of the place at all," Moor complained later. "But nobody could furnish either."

"Out into the enemy's country we marched," Lieutenant Colonel William Lincoln recalled. "The air is oppressively hot and close; the men are faint; and the ranks are getting thinned. Mount Jackson comes into sight; is reached; is passed; still our leader cries only 'Forward!' Still on; beyond support; past hope of help, if help be needed. So reckless seemed the movement that it was almost as if we left hope behind." In seven hours, Moor's men marched 21 miles with only a single, 10-minute rest. They camped just north of New Market on the 14th.

The heat and humidity of the day gave way that night to a pelting rain that would last well into the following day. The downpour caught General Imboden sleeping in the open, alongside the Valley Turnpike, four miles south of the town. "About two hours before daybreak I was aroused by the light of a tin lantern shining in my face," he recalled. "I was immediately accosted by General Breckinridge. He informed me his troops would reach that point before sunrise." It would be a day of battle.

Keenly aware that time was short, Breckinridge tried to get a quick sense of the terrain. He learned that the prospective battlefield was a small one, sharply delineated by natural features. Massanutten Mountain was less than two miles to the east, and a line of four hills just west of the pike extended one mile south and three and a half miles north of New Market. The North Fork of the Shenandoah angled in from the west and Smith's Creek from the east, until the two rain-swollen streams converged at Mount Jackson a few miles to the north.

Working swiftly in the steady rain, Breckinridge formed a line of battle across the Valley Turnpike. He sent Gabriel Wharton's brigade — augmented by two of Imboden's dismounted cavalry regiments — to the left, across the southernmost of the four hills. He placed two of John Echols' regiments, the 22nd and 23rd Virginia, astride the pike and held the third, the 62nd Virginia, in reserve alongside the VMI cadets. Imboden and the mounted 18th Virginia guarded the low, marshy ground between the pike and Smith's Creek.

With this accomplished by 8 a.m., Breckinridge ordered Imboden to prod Moor's line and try to draw an attack. But Moor refused the bait. With Sigel still in Woodstock and the rest of the Federal army strung out over the intervening 20 miles, Moor stayed put and sent for help.

Breckinridge prodded harder, moving a number of his guns north to the next crest, Shirley's Hill. Some of the fire from these guns fell short and hit the town. "Cannon balls and shells rolled and exploded in every direction," resident Jessie Rupert recalled.

"The air was filled with dust and smoke, and curses and shrieks." Terrified, she and her husband ripped up some floorboards and hid their infant son under their house, near its stone foundation.

When the Federals still showed no inclination to attack, Breckinridge ordered his infantry forward onto Shirley's Hill. If the Federals would not move, Breckinridge would. But first he had a special assignment for Imboden. He told the cavalryman to take the 18th Virginia and the horse artillery, ride to the east, circle behind the Federals and destroy the Mount Jackson Bridge, thus cutting the Federals off from reinforcement — and severing their main avenue of retreat.

By this time Brigadier General Julius Stahel, Sigel's cavalry commander, had arrived in New Market with the rest of the Federal troopers. Colonel Strother described Stahel contemptuously as a Hungarian exile and a former dancing master: "A little fellow, rather insignificant, looking for all the world like a traveling clerk in dress and figure." However, since he ranked Colonel Moor, Stahel took command.

Understrength and unsure when rein-

forcements would arrive, Stahel decided to fall back to New Market's northern outskirts. He aligned his men between the pike and the crest of Manor's Hill, north of Shirley's Hill, with a battery on each flank.

Shortly after 11 a.m., the Federals on Manor's Hill saw movement on Shirley's Hill. They were little concerned; as far as they knew, they were still dealing with only Imboden's cavalry. But then, a Federal gunner recalled, something odd happened to what he and his companions had thought was merely a fence across the top of Shirley's Hill. It moved. Instead of fence rails, the Federals found themselves staring at a row of bayonets. "A cold chill runs down our backs," the gunner wrote of the experience. He and his comrades realized they were facing Breckinridge's entire army — which now came down the hill "like a swarm of bees."

To offset the Federal guns pounding the slope of Shirley's Hill, Breckinridge ordered an unorthodox two-stage advance. The brigades of Echols and Wharton raced pell-mell to the bottom of the defile between the hills, where the enemy guns could not be depressed enough to reach them. After driving out the Federal skirmishers there, the Confederates paused to re-form their lines. The VMI cadets, however, did not get the word to hurry. They marched down the hill into the teeth of the Federal fire in parade-ground order, taking their first — and largely needless — casualties.

Breckinridge gave his men half an hour to rest before making the charge up Manor's Hill. Just then, around noon, General Sigel arrived on the field. Ever ready to call a retreat, he tried to persuade Moor and Stahel to fall back to Mount Jackson. When they resisted, Sigel said without enthusiasm, "We

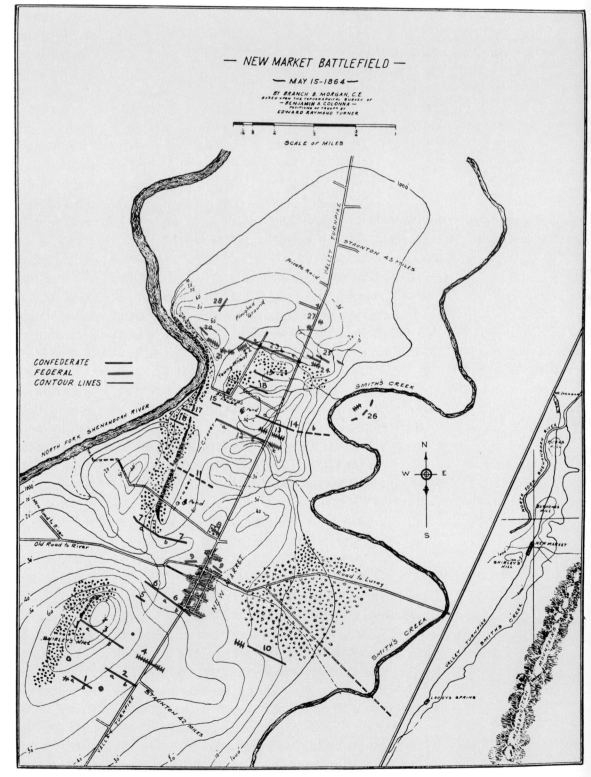

— NEW MARKET BATTLEFIELD —

— MAY 15-1864 —

BY BRANCH B. MORGAN, C.E.
BASED UPON THE TOPOGRAPHICAL SURVEY OF
— BENJAMIN A. COLONNA —
POSITIONS OF TROOPS BY
EDWARD RAYMOND TURNER

SCALE OF MILES

CONFEDERATE
FEDERAL
CONTOUR LINES

A battlefield map based on a survey by VMI's Benjamin Colonna, who fought at New Market as a cadet captain, details troop dispositions by number. With the cadets in the rear (1), the Confederates pushed north on the morning of May 15, forcing the Federal vanguard (9) to fall back from the crossroads. By early afternoon, Sigel had strung together a new formation, with the 34th Massachusetts on the right (20), Julius Stahel's cavalry on the left (25) and Augustus Moor's brigade in front (12). Moor's exposed line soon crumbled under pressure, and the Confederates closed in for the climactic drive.

Among the items borne into battle at New Market by the VMI cadets were this wooden canteen, Confederate flag and Spanish saber — displayed atop a leather trunk that was carried on the corps baggage wagon. Four cadets were detailed to stay behind and guard the wagon on May 15, but as the fighting escalated they hurried forward to join in; only one of the four escaped injury.

may as well fight them today as any day," and rode forward.

With 13 pieces of artillery firing in support, the Confederate line of battle began a steady climb up Manor's Hill. Demoralized by the bombardment and by the sight of the unexpectedly large attacking force, the regiment holding the center of Moor's line — his own 123rd Ohio — gave way long before the enemy reached it.

The men on either side of the 123rd were standing firm, but Sigel decided to pull back; four of his regiments were not up yet, and the enemy seemed more numerous than he had anticipated. He ordered his men to withdraw farther north, and Wharton's Confederates, to their surprise, found themselves in sole possession of Manor's Hill.

Sigel re-formed his men on Bushong's Hill, named for the family whose home and orchard were situated atop it. He deployed two lines, thinking to slow the Confederate advance with the first line while he fed arriving units into the second. The forward line — the less-than-stalwart 123rd Ohio, the 18th Connecticut and Captain Albert von Kleiser's battery — was deployed in the shallow depression between Manor's and Bushong's Hills. The main line formed up north of the Bushong house and orchard. Two other batteries held the right on the hill's crest. The infantry — including the 54th Pennsylvania, which had just arrived on

the field — extended to the pike and Stahel's understrength cavalry sat east of the pike.

Sigel's errors were accumulating fast. His army actually outnumbered the Confederates, but his combat line was outnumbered by 3 to 2. Thus, his advanced infantry line could be overlapped on both flanks by the attackers. He compounded that mistake by deploying his cavalry with its left in the air and with no room because of the difficult terrain to mount an effective charge.

Breckinridge paused on Manor's Hill to restore his formations and place his artillery; he massed 10 of his 13 guns ahead of his main line, east of the Valley Turnpike, facing Moor's left and Stahel's right. He took a few minutes to ride along his lines, steadying the men with his commanding presence. Then, stationing himself near the forward guns, he ordered the infantry to charge.

The rain-soaked battle flags hung limply, and the men's feet caught in the ankle-deep mud. A mild wind pushed thick clouds of acrid cannon smoke over the battlefield, obscuring some of the attackers.

The hapless 123rd Ohio fired a single volley at the Confederates and broke for the rear. The 18th Connecticut and von Kleiser's battery, their left thus exposed, had no choice but to fall back as well. On came the Confederates, grimly closing with the main Federal body. As the tension mounted, the Federals of the 12th West Virginia, in reserve to the rear, panicked and fired a volley into the backs of their comrades, wounding several of them.

Meanwhile, Imboden and his cavalry, on their circuit around the Federal left, had worked their way through some woods on a rise east of Smith's Creek. Suddenly they found themselves overlooking the left flank of Stahel's cavalry. Just as Breckinridge launched his charge on Bushong's Hill, Imboden ordered his artillery to open fire on what he described as "acres of men and horses." The effect on the enemy, Imboden reported, "was magical. The first discharge of the guns threw his whole body of cavalry into confusion."

Then the tide of the battle unexpectedly began to run against the Confederates. When Wharton's men came within musket range of Sigel's main line, just north of the Bushong house, their charge stalled. At the same time, Echols' advance along the pike was halted by fire from Stahel's troopers, who had recovered from Imboden's surprise bombardment. For a few minutes the two armies stood face to face, shooting it out, neither side able to gain an advantage. Then disaster threatened the Confederate center.

Von Kleiser's battery blew a hole in Wharton's line between the 51st and 62nd Virginia. A staff officer galloped up to Breckinridge, shouting that the day would be lost if the Federals spotted the gap and counterattacked. Breckinridge thought of extending his lines, but his men were pinned down.

"Put in the cadets," urged the officer.

"They are only children," answered Breckinridge. Then he asked aloud: "Will they stand?" Moments later, Breckinridge gave the command: "Put the boys in, and may God forgive me for the order."

The cadets rose with a cheer and surged forward into the Federal shot and shell. Topping a slight rise in the ground that had shielded them, the yelling boys ran toward the Bushong house, one after another of them going down under the Federal fire. One youngster clawed at the grass in his death agony. Another ripped the shirt from his chest to display his mortal wound to the sky as he toppled backward into the mud. Their commander, Lieutenant Colonel Scott Shipp, reported with justifiable pride: "The alignment of the battalion under this terrible fire, which strewed the ground with killed and wounded for more than a mile on open ground, would have been creditable even on a field day."

The cadets reached their objective, a rail fence north of the Bushong orchard. On command, the boys knelt, raised their dripping muskets and fired a volley. As a Federal officer recalled, "A streak of fire and smoke flashed across the field." The gap in the Confederate line was closed.

But Wharton's brigade was still in peril because its right, now held by the cadets, remained exposed; Echols' stalled line was several hundred yards to the rear. And now Stahel launched his 1,000 troopers in a charge against Echols' 1,100 infantrymen.

Echols' two regiments were ably commanded. The 22nd Virginia was led by Colonel George S. Patton — whose grandson and namesake would command the U.S. Third Army in World War II — and Lieutenant Colonel Clarence Derrick headed the 23rd Virginia. As the Federal cavalry thundered toward Derrick's center, the two colonels quickly improvised a defense. The men on Derrick's left and center jammed themselves shoulder to shoulder into small squares from which they could fire outward in all directions; the right of Derrick's line wheeled inward to take the approaching cavalrymen with flanking fire. Patton's men wheeled in the opposite direction. The Federal troopers found themselves galloping into a deadly corridor with a closed end.

Nor was that the worst of it. Imboden's

Amid bursting shells and flashes of lightning, the cadets charge through the smoke toward Albert von Kleiser's battery in this heroic painting, displayed at VMI's Jackson Memorial Hall. A Federal officer who was near the battery at the time marveled: "I think it would have been impossible to eject from six guns more missiles than these boys faced in their wild charge."

For 17-year-old cadet Thomas G. Jefferson (*left*), his first engagement at New Market was his last. Shot in the chest, he was found by his roommate that evening on the battlefield and carried by wagon to the nearby home of Eliza Clinedinst (*opposite*), under whose roof he died three days later.

Jaqueline (Jack) B. Stanard, one of the cadets who left the baggage wagon to fight with his comrades, was wounded alongside Jefferson and died at a field hospital a few hours later. Word of Stanard's fate was conveyed to his home near Orange Court House by telegram (*above*) the day after the battle.

guns, in the woods across Smith's Creek, had resumed firing on Stahel's left. Breckinridge, grasping the situation, ran his guns forward along the pike and had them blaze away at Stahel's right with canister. Unnerved by the ferocious artillery fire coming from two directions, the Federal cavalrymen reversed direction in midcharge and galloped for the rear.

Belatedly, Sigel tried to organize an infantry counterattack to block Wharton's advancing troops. But in the excitement he lapsed into German, and many of his shouted orders were incomprehensible to his American subordinates. By the time the Federal troops started moving forward, it was too late. Wharton's line had stabilized; Patton and Derrick had changed front to face the new threat; and Breckinridge had redirected his massed artillery.

The men of the 1st West Virginia moved out from Sigel's center before the regiments on either flank were ready. They struggled forward for 100 yards, then broke for the rear. To their left, the 54th Pennsylvania also began retreating. Only the 34th Massachu-

setts on the Federal right doggedly pressed forward, taking more than 200 casualties, almost half the regiment's strength, in a few minutes. Colonel George D. Wells tried to order a retreat, but in the deafening roar of the guns, "they either could not hear or would not heed the order," he said. In desperation Wells ran forward, grabbed the color-bearer and bodily turned him around.

Ironically, Wells began his retreat just as the Confederate 51st Virginia began to fall back from the orchard fence, dismayed by the determined advance of the men from Massachusetts. But the 26th Virginia quickly came up from its reserve position to bolster the 51st and together they regained the line to the left of the VMI cadets, who were stubbornly holding their ground.

Then, with no general order given — or

Young Eliza Clinedinst — known to grateful VMI veterans after her marriage as Mother Crim — opened her doors to the wounded and hungry alike in the wake of the fighting at New Market. Among those she comforted was a 15-year-old cadet who, though unscathed, seemed helpless after the ordeal of battle. "He wanted his bread spread with preserves," she recalled. "He sat down just like a little child to eat from Mother's hand."

possible, with the roar of battle now augmented by the renewed fury of the rainstorm — the entire Confederate line rose up and charged. The cadets drove into the gap between the 54th Pennsylvania and the 34th Massachusetts, punishing both units with enfilading fire. They advanced so quickly that von Kleiser had to abandon one of his guns, and the cadets ensured their place in legend by capturing a field piece in their first battle. "A shout, a rush, and the day was won," Colonel Shipp later exulted.

On the cadets' left, the combined forces of the 26th and 51st Virginia smashed into the 34th Massachusetts, delivering such a concentrated fire that the Federal regiment's color-bearer, mortally wounded by one bullet, was struck by three more before his body hit the ground.

Sigel tried desperately to hold his men in place, but it was too late. His army disinte-grated as the Confederates swarmed over Bushong's Hill. Sigel's provost marshal, Lieutenant Colonel William Starr, tried valiantly to stop the Federal flight. A rifle ball killed the horse under him, and another horse he tried to mount panicked and threw him; before he could mount a third, a squad of fleeing cavalrymen ran him down.

Sigel's army might have been destroyed but for the timely appearance of Captain Henry A. DuPont. Arriving from Mount Jackson with his single battery, DuPont hastily strung his guns along the pike by sections, with 500 yards between each pair of guns. The lead section was to fire until almost overrun, then dash to the rear of the line to wait for its turn to come again. DuPont's men kept up a steady fire for four miles, winning precious time for Sigel's retreating army. Afterwards, DuPont would bitterly recall: "I had to depend entirely upon myself and did not receive a single order, either directly or indirectly, from any military superior."

The moment he saw that the day was won, Breckinridge rode over to the cadets on Bushong's Hill. By this time, reported Shipp, the boys were not only exhausted but also "wet, hungry, and many of them shoeless — for they had lost their shoes and socks in the deep mud."

"Well done, Virginians," Breckinridge said to them proudly. "Well done, men." Then he ordered them to fall out, and as one of the youths recalled, "he turned and rode away, taking with him the heart of every one of us." But the cadets had paid a high price for their moment of glory; 10 of them had been killed and 47 wounded, almost one fourth of their number.

Breckinridge intended to bag Sigel's en-

The 34th Massachusetts, fiercely engaged at New Market, had done most of its service in camp near Washington, D.C. (*below*), leading one officer to wonder how men "who almost never before had heard the rebel yell" could be so cool under fire. Even after the capture of their commander, Lieutenant Colonel William Lincoln (*left*), they held out around their bullet-shredded battle flags.

tire army. But before he could begin the chase, Imboden rode up with frustrating news; he had been unable to recross Smith's Creek and destroy the bridge at Mount Jackson. Thinking Sigel might try to make a stand at the river anyway, Breckinridge ordered his men forward.

Earlier in the day, Sigel had sent two of Moor's Ohio regiments to Mount Jackson but had forgotten to order them up to New Market until too late. When Sigel met them a little after 6 p.m. at Rude's Hill, halfway between the two towns, he considered trying to hold the position. But he did not have the heart for it.

Instead, Sigel marched his men across the Shenandoah River and headed north, neglecting to leave a rear guard to prepare the bridge for burning and hold it until Captain DuPont's battery could arrive. When DuPont and his weary men finally reached the bridge, they found it "absolutely deserted." The furious DuPont had to waste precious time setting the wooden span on fire before following the retreating army.

South of the Mount Jackson Bridge, as evening fell, the victors celebrated so loudly that they could be heard for miles. Breckinridge's adjutant, Major J. Stoddard Johnson, remembered cheering "such as had not been heard in the Valley since Stonewall Jackson had led them."

The victory deserved its full-throated celebration. Breckinridge had not destroyed Sigel's army, but he had crippled it. At the cost of 43 Confederate dead, 474 wounded and three missing, he had inflicted far greater losses on the Federals: 96 dead, 520 wounded and 225 captured or missing. He had saved for the time at least the principal

source of rations for Robert E. Lee's army — a fact underscored that very evening by a dispatch from General Lee to all the Confederate quartermasters in Virginia. "Borrow all the corn you can from citizens and send me at once. If persons holding corn will not let you have it, impress it. I presume an impressment will not be necessary when the magnitude of the stake is thought of. Answer me at once what you can do."

Eager as they were for a favorable omen, many Confederates saw an almost mystical significance in the fact that Breckinridge's victory had come on the first anniversary of Stonewall Jackson's funeral. The Richmond newspapers compared Breckinridge with the hero of the 1862 Shenandoah Campaign, and soon the victor of New Market was being hailed as "the new Jackson, who had been sent to guard the Valley and redeem it from the occupation of the enemy."

But with the immediate threat to his life line repulsed, Lee could not afford the luxury of leaving Breckinridge in the Valley. Earlier in the War, when the Federals had been driven back in the Shenandoah, they had spent several dazed months pondering what to do next. Assuming the pattern would hold, and much in need of a fighting general, Lee ordered Breckinridge to join him at Hanover Junction.

But this time the Valley would have no respite, for General Grant was imposing a faster tempo on the War. When chief of staff Henry W. Halleck suggested that the incompetent Sigel be replaced by Major General David Hunter, an aging but aggressive officer, Grant eagerly concurred. The transfer took place on May 19, the day Breckinridge left the Valley.

"Black Dave's" Orgy of Fire

"Had Hunter moved on Lynchburg with energy, that place would have fallen before it was possible for me to get there."

LIEUTENANT GENERAL JUBAL A. EARLY, C.S.A.

2

Major General David Hunter burned with inner rage. Grim and energetic, Hunter usually projected a tense quietude, but he was capable of erupting into sudden, violent fury. His advancing years — he turned 62 shortly after taking command of the Federal Department of West Virginia in May of 1864 — had neither mellowed nor marked him. His hair was so black — "straight, coarse and of midnight hue," one visitor to his headquarters remembered — that many of his men were convinced he dyed it. "His complexion was swarthy," wrote the visitor, "and his lineaments somewhat suggestive of an Indian."

During Hunter's long military career, his disputatious ways had kept him in constant turmoil. He was said to have killed two fellow officers in duels. Once Hunter went so far as to challenge his commanding officer, and for that offense he was tried by court martial and sentenced to be dismissed from the service. Only the intervention of President John Quincy Adams saved his career.

Hunter became a bitter opponent of slavery, and on this issue he focused all his toxic anger. Although he was a member of a prominent Virginia family, he declared that the participation of Virginians in suppressing John Brown's raid on the U.S. Armory at Harpers Ferry in 1859 justified the destruction of the state.

Posted to Kansas in 1860, Hunter ignored the usual restraints on Army officers and involved himself deeply in the bitter political debates raging there, even corresponding with presidential candidate Abraham Lincoln on the prospects for secession. After the election of 1860, Hunter was invited to accompany the President-elect on his journey to Washington. As a result of that intimacy, Hunter felt free to refer his military problems directly to Lincoln.

After recovering from a wound received at Bull Run, Hunter was promoted to major general and sent to the Department of the West. When the department commander, Major General John C. Frémont, was relieved (one of Frémont's transgressions had been to emancipate prematurely the slaves in his department), Hunter was put in charge. But within a few days, the department was split and Hunter was relegated to a lesser command back in Kansas. Hunter bitterly complained to Lincoln that he was being "humiliated, insulted and disgraced."

Hunter had misread the President's amiability. "It is difficult to answer so ugly a letter in a good temper," Lincoln responded. "I am, as you intimate, losing much of the great confidence I placed in you, not from any act or omission of yours but from the flood of grumbling dispatches and letters I have seen from you since." The order would stand, said Lincoln, and Hunter would be well advised to do his duty without further complaint: "You are adopting the best possible way to ruin yourself."

Neither the letter from Lincoln nor the downfall of Frémont made any impression

This regulation Confederate cavalry kepi was worn by Captain George J. Pratt of the 18th Virginia Cavalry, who fought in the battles of New Market and Piedmont in the spring of 1864. As an economy, the brim was made of inexpensive oilcloth instead of fine leather.

on Hunter. Later, upon receiving command of the Department of the South with headquarters at Federally occupied Hilton Head, South Carolina, he immediately took it upon himself to start freeing slaves. He soon announced the formation of the War's first black regiment — the 1st South Carolina Volunteers. An exasperated Lincoln countermanded Hunter's emancipation orders and the general was recalled to Washington, where he spent almost a year sitting on commissions and boards before being sent to the Shenandoah. The Confederate government, horrified at the prospect of armed blacks, declared Hunter an outlaw who, if captured, "shall not be regarded as a prisoner of war, but held in close confinement for execution as a felon."

None of this daunted Hunter. Artillery Captain Henry DuPont recalled that Hunter had pressed Washington, in 1863, for permission to organize a "general arming of the negroes and a general destruction of all the property of the slaveholders in the South." DuPont wrote that Hunter was "dominated by prejudices and antipathies so intense and so violent as to render him at times quite incapable of taking a fair and unbiased view of many military and political situations."

Despite his excesses, Hunter was an experienced, well-trained officer who looked especially good by comparison with his predecessor. "We can afford to lose such a battle as New Market," concluded Colonel David Strother ruefully, "to get rid of such a mistake as Major General Sigel."

In the main, that view would be confirmed by the whirlwind events of the succeeding month, during which Hunter would accomplish everything that Sigel had been asked to do, and more. But that substantial achievement would be marred by Hunter's savagery toward pro-South civilians — and negated in the end by a spectacular loss of nerve.

Hunter took firm hold of a command he found to be "utterly demoralized and stampeded." From his headquarters — an imposing stone house called Belle Grove, on an estate north of Strasburg — he sent Sigel north to command the reserves guarding the B&O and ordered Brigadier General Crook to leave his West Virginia sanctuary and "move immediately on Staunton."

Hunter also weeded Sigel's cronies from his staff, appointing Strother chief of staff and making DuPont chief of artillery. He tried but failed to replace Sigel's two division commanders, Julius Stahel and Jeremiah Sullivan. Then on May 26, just five days after taking command, Hunter marched the rejuvenated Army of the Shenandoah, now 8,500 strong, southward once again.

Grant wanted Hunter to join Crook and move against the rail hubs of Charlottesville and Lynchburg. General Halleck relayed the instructions, telling Hunter to destroy the railroads "beyond the possibility of repair for weeks; then, either return to your original base or join Grant, via Gordonsville."

General Hunter began a campaign of destruction long before he reached a railroad. When on May 24 a Federal wagon train was fired on near Newtown, eight miles south of Winchester, Hunter sent a cavalry detachment to burn the house from which the shots came. He ordered the troopers to announce a tough, new policy: If the incident were repeated, "the commanding general will cause to be burned every rebel house within five miles of the place at which the firing occurs."

Hunter's so-called retaliation order was unusual, to say the least, in the Eastern Theater, where the armies of both sides were under orders to safeguard civilians and private property. "Indiscriminate marauding should be avoided," Grant had told Sigel. "Nothing should be taken not absolutely necessary for the troops, except when captured from an armed enemy."

Hunter felt justified in stretching these orders because he was convinced that the Confederate cavalry leaders — John Mosby, Hanse McNeill and Harry Gilmor — were not military officers at all but outlaws beyond the pale of civilized warfare, a conclusion that Captain DuPont, for one, called "absolutely untenable." Hunter wreaked his vengeance on pro-Confederate civilians with an enthusiasm that sometimes disturbed his own men. Every day, whether or not any Federals had been shot at, dark columns of smoke from burning homes marked the army's southward course. More than once Hunter put the torch to houses owned by his Virginia relatives. With pungent accuracy the Federal troops began calling their glowering commander "Black Dave."

Near Strasburg, a farmer's house that was rumored to be a meeting place for partisans went up in smoke; the next day, a captain was sent to burn a house said to belong to another supposed partisan. Strother recalled that the officer "came back to report that he had found there a woman with three little children and they had nowhere to go, so his heart failed him and he came away without executing the order." Hunter reprimanded the captain and then laughed, declaring that the house was such a mean affair it was not worth burning.

Marching through Woodstock on May 29,

Hunter stopped the column and had the jail searched, "evidently seeking an apology to burn something," Strother wrote. Finding no Federal prisoners, Hunter thought he might burn the town's hotel anyway, but Strother talked him out of it.

Then Hunter received word that another Federal wagon train had been attacked near Newtown. Enraged, he sent a detachment from the 1st New York Cavalry to burn "every house, store and outbuilding in that place." But the detachment commander, Major Joseph K. Stearns, faced objections not only from the residents — who pleaded that they had nothing to do with Mosby's men — but also from the New Yorkers, some of whom announced flatly that they would not obey the order. Stearns decided not to harm the town, and returned to face the wrath of his commanding general.

On the 30th of May, the army reached New Market and surveyed the ghastly vestiges of the battle that had just been fought. "In a slight hollow of the field," wrote an officer of the 34th Massachusetts, "the bodies of our dead, thrown indiscriminately into a pile, and but partially covered with earth, presented a sickening sight. Feet, arms and heads were protruding at all points of this festering mass." Colonel Strother noticed that the dead horses had received more diligent attention; they had been "carefully skinned and their shoes taken off."

A burial detail interred the dead properly, and the advance continued. On June 2 the army camped on a hill overlooking Harrisonburg, and Hunter learned that the enemy was eight miles south, at Mount Crawford, where the Valley Turnpike crossed the North River. Progress thus far had been easy. Now he would have to fight.

Major General David Hunter, the new commander of Federal forces in the Shenandoah Valley, had no respect for the division commanders he inherited, Generals Jeremiah Sullivan and Julius Stahel. In a letter to Grant, he complained that Sullivan and Stahel were "not worth one cent."

ment of Southwestern Virginia — now including East Tennessee.

It was conceded that there was no more caustic a personality in the Confederate Army than Jones. He had the look of an Old Testament prophet, with glittering eyes framed by a bushy beard below and a balding head above. Those who knew him dated his antisocial behavior to a tragic day in 1852 when, as a young Regular Army cavalry officer returning by ship from California, he had his bride of two months swept from his arms to her death during a storm at sea.

Jones resigned from the Army in 1857 and returned to his native Washington County in southwestern Virginia. There he lived as a hermit farmer, known to his neighbors even then as Grumble. When the War began, he rode out of the hills to take command of a volunteer company called the Washington Mounted Rifles.

"Ragged! Ragged!" Jones would shriek at his amateur troopers in his high-pitched voice. "It must be smooth! Some of you damned farmhands haven't got out of the bulrushes!" Endlessly he drilled his men and swore at them; but nevertheless he earned their respect. One recruit, a young lawyer named John S. Mosby, admired Jones's ability and wrote later that the training was "a good course of discipline."

Paradoxically, Jones the stickler for drill was slovenly in appearance; he simply tacked his officer's insignia on his ragged homespun coat, which he wore over a hickory shirt and bluejeans. His indifference to dress extended to that of his men; when they saw a shipment of uniforms he had obtained for them, wrote Mosby, "there was almost a mutiny. They were a sort of dun color and came from the penitentiary." Yet Jones somehow got his

The departure of Major General John Breckinridge had left the Confederate forces in western Virginia with no commander and no instructions. It appeared that the dour Brigadier General William E. (Grumble) Jones was the senior officer remaining. On May 20 he had fired off a waspish, one-line telegram to Richmond: "Must I assume command of Department of Western Virginia?" Three days later orders were issued, placing Jones at the head of a new Depart-

On a wooded ridge overlooking the Shenandoah Valley *(below)*, Colonel John S. Mosby *(in red-lined cape)* and his Rangers prepare to attack the Federals. Scores of energetic young Southerners were attracted to the independent cavalry chieftain, seen sitting jauntily among some of his men *(inset)*, wearing his customary plumed hat. As one of Mosby's men explained: "There was a fascination in the life of a Ranger. The changing scenes, the wild adventure, and even the dangers themselves exerted a seductive influence."

recruits equipped with new Sharps breech-loading carbines.

Jones went on to command a company in the 1st Virginia Cavalry under the dashing and dandified Lieutenant Colonel James E. B. (Jeb) Stuart, with whom he was utterly incompatible. They clashed repeatedly until, in September of 1863, Jones committed what one officer described as "a flagrant piece of official insolence." Jones was found guilty of insubordination by a court martial and sent to western Virginia, away from Stuart. Not visibly affected by his troubles, Jones simply went on fighting, terrifying his enemies in battle, his men in camp.

Jones was first of all a soldier. On learning in May of 1864 of Stuart's death, he was distraught. "By God, Martin," he cried to his adjutant. "You know I had little love for Stuart and he had just as little for me. But that is the greatest loss this Army has ever sustained since the death of Jackson!" That same month Jones was being considered for promotion to major general, and an inspecting officer reported favorably: "Notwithstanding all his grumbling, he is a fine officer."

In the wake of Breckinridge's departure, Jones found himself facing a nightmarish reprise of the crisis of a few weeks earlier. On May 27 General John Imboden reported from New Market that Hunter was advancing from Strasburg: "His cavalry outnumbers ours two to one, his infantry four to one, his artillery four to one. There is no point this side of Mount Crawford where I can successfully resist him."

Robert E. Lee sent Jones essentially the same order he had sent Breckinridge in late April, instructing him on May 30 to "get all the available forces you can and move at once to Imboden's assistance to defend the Val-ley." That same day, Crook's Federals marched out of Meadow Bluff and headed for Staunton to rendezvous with Hunter.

Hunter moved faster than Sigel had, and Jones had even fewer men with which to respond than had Breckinridge. The harried Imboden threw up fortifications on June 2 and prepared to make a stand behind the North River at Mount Crawford. The next day Jones's three understrength infantry regiments and a brigade of mounted infantry commanded by Brigadier General John C. Vaughn began to file into the Mount Crawford position, swelling the Confederate force to 5,000. On the 4th, Jones himself arrived — and so did the Federals.

Hunter still had 8,500 men with him; when Crook's 10,000 appeared, his numerical advantage would be overwhelming. But Hunter did not know Crook's whereabouts. Without Crook, Hunter thought the Confederate position at Mount Crawford too strong for a frontal assault. He decided to flank the Confederates out of their prepared defenses. Instead of marching southwest up the Valley Turnpike, he headed southeast toward Port Republic. From there the Federal cavalry could take Waynesboro, 15 miles farther south, sever the Virginia Central and, with Staunton thus cut off, bring Jones to battle on more favorable ground.

The movement caught Jones by surprise. But at Port Republic, where the North, South and Middle Rivers converge to form the South Fork of the Shenandoah, the Federals had to throw a pontoon bridge across the rain-swollen waters. "There seemed to be no one of the engineers who understood how to put up the canvas pontoons," recalled Strother. "It was awkwardly done and so slow that it was evident that we would lose all the benefit of our early march."

The crossing was not completed until 6 p.m. By that time Jones knew what was afoot. Hunter's planned dash to Waynesboro was now out of the question. His army would have to march directly on Staunton and would have to fight Jones to get there — but not this day. Another hard rain had begun to fall, and the drenched Federals camped for the night a mile south of Port Republic.

Skirmishing began shortly after sunrise on Sunday, June 5, exactly three weeks after the Federal defeat at New Market. The 1st New York Cavalry pushed southward along the East road, and Imboden's men took on the now-familiar task of trying to hold off a superior force until the Confederate infantry had time to organize a defense. This time they could not stem the tide for long, and they had to fall back. The Federals captured 70 men from the 18th Virginia Cavalry, including one of General Imboden's brothers, Captain Frank Imboden. (Another brother, George, was the colonel commanding the 18th; a third, James, was its sergeant major.)

As Imboden backed away from the skirmish, he was startled to come upon Jones's main force at the little village of Piedmont, a single street of wood-frame houses, eight miles south of Port Republic. The previous day Jones and Imboden had agreed that their stand should be made closer to Staunton. But Jones subsequently had received orders from Lee to engage Hunter quickly, before Crook arrived. Thus, he decided to move farther north, to Piedmont, where he deployed his infantry regiments on a series of wooded hills in front of the village, between the East road and a bluff overlooking the Middle River. The troops hastily erected log-and-rail breastworks along the tree line.

Confederate Brigadier General William E. (Grumble) Jones was at first hated by his men because of his cantankerous nature and rigid discipline. When the troops were not in action, Jones drilled them daily; he designated each Saturday "saber-grinding day," even though sabers were rarely used in combat.

About a mile to the rear, a second line of defenses was set up at the edge of a stand of timber on the opposite side of the village. The second line, manned by Vaughn's mounted infantry and Imboden's cavalry, extended almost two miles eastward from the road across a little valley to Round Top Hill.

Hunter deployed Sullivan's division west of the road with Augustus Moor's brigade on the right, and Joseph Thoburn's on the left. DuPont massed his 22 guns near the road. Stahel's cavalry was held in reserve.

Hunter took time out to make a speech to the men of the 18th Connecticut, telling them they were about to get a chance to make up for their sorry performance at New Market. "They didn't seem much elated with the prospect," recalled Strother, "and scarcely got up a decent cheer in response."

At midmorning Moor's skirmishers drove the Confederate pickets into their breastworks — then backed away in surprise as the defenders stormed out at them, screaming derisively: "New Market! New Market!" The counterattack was stopped only after fierce fighting. While Moor got the rest of his brigade into position for another attack and

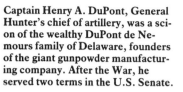
Captain Henry A. DuPont, General Hunter's chief of artillery, was a scion of the wealthy DuPont de Nemours family of Delaware, founders of the giant gunpowder manufacturing company. After the War, he served two terms in the U.S. Senate.

York Heavy Artillery, serving now as infantry, charged almost to the Confederate defenses; "here the soldiers fought desperately and at some disadvantage, being entirely in the open field." Ely pleaded for artillery support. In response, DuPont brought forward two guns, unlimbered them 500 yards from the enemy and opened fire with solid shot. The guns, reported Ely, "did excellent service in knocking the rail pens to splinters amid great slaughter." But no decisive advantage was gained, and the 18th Connecticut and the 5th New York artillerymen remained stalled in the open.

They fought obstinately. In Ely's words, "Many were falling under the hot fire. Our colors were riddled by three cannon shot and thirteen bullets, and all of our color guard but one killed or wounded." Whatever damage the Connecticut regiment's reputation had suffered at New Market was being repaired at Piedmont.

But at last Moor's brigade, having suffered more than 150 casualties, had to fall back. "This seemed to encourage the enemy," DuPont recalled. The Confederates, "with ear-splitting yells, made a most determined assault upon our whole line."

Hunter was becoming discouraged. The Confederate line had reacted like a prodded snake to every Federal initiative, lashing out and fighting the attackers to a standstill. Now he saw movement that suggested the enemy was massing for a counterattack on his right. Hunter ordered his wagons turned around in preparation for a withdrawal. But first he would try one more assault.

His target would be a flaw in the Confederate lines — an interval of several hundred yards between Jones's right and Vaughn's left. Jones himself was not worried about the

Thoburn aligned to Moor's left, the troops came under heavy but inaccurate fire from the Confederate artillery. Captain DuPont concentrated the fire of the Federal guns on one after another of the enemy batteries until, he wrote, the Confederates were "compelled to abandon their position and fall back rather precipitately." By 11:30 a.m., the Confederate fire had ceased entirely.

At 1 p.m. Moor attacked again. Colonel William G. Ely, commanding the 18th Connecticut on the extreme Federal right, reported that his regiment and the 5th New

Ignoring his wounded arm, Federal cavalry chief Julius Stahel, shown at far right before his promotion to major general, is handed his saber before resuming the attack at Piedmont. For his valor, Stahel won the Medal of Honor and the respect of his fellow officers; many of them had dismissed the Hungarian-born officer as a foreign poseur.

gap because his cavalry could charge the flank of any Federal turning movement. But to be safe, he began pulling his line back to the crossroads to join Vaughn's.

Hunter, with his eye on that inviting gap, had set Thoburn's brigade in motion. Leaving skirmishers in place to mask their intentions, the 34th Massachusetts and the 54th Pennsylvania pulled back into some woods. From there they marched across the road to the southeast, into a treelined hollow that led directly to the opening in the Confederate ranks. The Federals approached to within 700 yards of the enemy's forward line without drawing much response; when told about the Federal movement, Jones, probably thinking of the corrective measures he had already ordered, answered that there was nothing to fear.

Jones's assessment was wrong. "The critical point of the day had arrived," said Strother. The 54th Pennsylvania, according to its colonel, Jacob M. Campbell, fired a volley and "immediately charged into the woods on the right flank and rear of the enemy's entrenched position. Here for a short time a most desperate struggle took place, bayonets and clubbed guns were used on both sides, and many hand-to-hand encounters took place."

To the left of the Pennsylvanians, the 34th Massachusetts opened fire "at scant 20 yards distance," Lieutenant Colonel William Lincoln wrote later in the regiment's official history. "The enemy broke back into the woods in some confusion; our line advanced cheering and the day was seemingly ours."

But Jones, working furiously, rallied his defenders and sent orders to Vaughn and Imboden to counterattack. Then he rushed to a small reserve force he had posted on the road

and personally led it, into the left flank of the 34th Massachusetts. "In less than five minutes," Lieutenant Colonel Lincoln recalled, "we lost our major, adjutant, senior captain, and 55 men killed or wounded." But the Confederates suffered a more grievous loss: Grumble Jones, struck in the head by a bullet, fell dead from his horse.

Meanwhile Moor's battle-weary brigade moved forward yet again toward the Confederate left, supported this time by Stahel and the bulk of the Federal cavalry division. Those troopers who carried Spencer repeating rifles were ordered to dismount and advance on foot on Moor's right.

A piece of shrapnel struck Stahel in the arm. Weakened by shock and loss of blood, he nevertheless had himself lifted onto a horse to lead his mounted men in a charge on the crumbling Confederate position. For his boldness and courage, the much-maligned former dancing master would be awarded the Congressional Medal of Honor.

The Confederates on the right, demoralized by the death of Jones, fell back in disorder before the 34th Massachusetts, the 54th Pennsylvania and the rest of the Federal cavalry, led by Colonel John E. Wynkoop. The 2,000 horsemen commanded by Vaughn and Imboden — almost half the Confederate force — sat on their horses and watched the destruction of the infantry without making a move. Vaughn pleaded afterward that he had been ordered by Jones to hold his position until he received further orders. The orders never came; in the confusion, the courier sent by Jones could not find either Vaughn or Imboden.

There was nothing for the Confederate infantry to do but run. Within moments, the entire Federal army sensed victory: At

Hunter's headquarters, "the earth shook with the roar of guns and musketry, and the fresh, hearty cheers rose with the smoke," Strother recalled. "Back rolled the cheers from the front. Stretcher men, ambulance drivers, wounded men, butchers, bummers and all took up the shout."

The Federal cavalry pursued the defeated Confederates only about a mile, and Vaughn and Imboden were able to lead their men south and then east to Waynesboro; from there they slipped through the Blue Ridge at Rockfish Gap. Although the bulk of the enemy force had escaped, Hunter was satisfied with the day's work and decided to camp that night on the field. At a cost of only 420 casualties, the Federals had dealt the Confederate army a smashing blow, killing or wounding about 600 men and taking more than a thousand prisoners.

Earlier that afternoon, as the battlefield was growing quiet, Strother had been sent to confirm that Jones had indeed been killed.

"I found a crowd around a body coarsely clothed in a dirty gray suit without any trappings or military insignia about it," he wrote. But Strother, a Virginian himself, was not deceived. "He had on a pair of fine military boots well worn and fine woolen underclothes perfectly clean and new. His hands were small and white, and his features, high white forehead, brown beard, and long hair indicated the gentleman and man of the upper class."

For the first time in the War, a Federal army had the run of the Shenandoah Valley. On June 6, the day after the battle, Hunter marched his men into Staunton and un-

leashed an orgy of destruction. This time he confined his attentions to property of military significance — storehouses, mills, workshops and railroad facilities.

But while the military property was being wrecked, unrestrained looting began in Staunton, carried out, in Strother's words, by "a mixed mob of Federal soldiers, Negroes, Secessionists, mulatto women" and "the riffraff of the town. At the Virginia Hotel Hospital, the provost guard were knocking the heads out of numerous barrels of apple brandy. The precious stream was running over the curbstones in cascades and rushing down the gutters with floating chips,

Confederate Colonel Edwin G. Lee (*above*) did his best to save the stockpile of supplies at Staunton (*right*). He rushed what he could to General Vaughn at Waynesboro and sent other matériel to Lynchburg and across the Blue Ridge into Nelson County; then he invited the citizens to the rest.

paper, horse dung and dead rats. This luscious mixture was greedily drunk by dozens of soldiers and vagabonds on their hands and knees and their mouths in the gutter while the more nice were setting their canteens to catch it as it flowed over the curbs."

On June 8, Crook and the Army of the Kanawha arrived from the west. They had been marching for more than a week, tearing up the railroad and skirmishing repeatedly with Confederate cavalry under Colonel William L. Jackson — called "Mudwall," General Crook explained sarcastically, "in contradistinction to Stonewall Jackson." The West Virginians were still short of supplies,

and the shoes of many of the men were falling to pieces. But their needs were readily met by the bounty from Staunton's storerooms.

With his force now increased to 18,000 men and 30 guns, Hunter prepared to march eastward, across the Blue Ridge to his next objective. He relieved the wounded Stahel and put his 1st Cavalry Division under the command of Brigadier General Alfred N. Duffié, a former officer in the French army. And in place of the stalwart Colonel Moor, whose term of enlistment was up, Colonel George D. Wells of the 34th Massachusetts took command of the 1st Infantry Division's 1st Brigade.

In eastern Virginia, a month of unprecedented slaughter had reached its climax at Cold Harbor, where Lee had dealt Grant a costly rebuff. As the awesome pressures of this struggle intensified, the Valley and its critical railroads were continually on the minds of both commanders.

As the two great armies paused to recover from Cold Harbor, Lee sent Breckinridge and his division west again, with President Davis' concurrence, to reclaim the Shenandoah from Hunter. Grant, meanwhile, sent two divisions of cavalry under Major General Philip H. Sheridan to join Hunter at Charlottesville and, in Grant's words, "break up the railroad connection between Richmond and the Shenandoah Valley and Lynchburg." Once this had been accomplished, the combined forces of Sheridan and Hunter were to march east and help Grant complete the encirclement of Richmond.

Lee countered by dispatching Major General Wade Hampton, who was proving himself worthy of taking the place of Jeb Stuart, with two cavalry divisions to fend off Sheridan. Hampton succeeded in doing this in a series of hotly contested skirmishes near Trevilian Station.

Lee could ill afford to detach these troops. His Army of Northern Virginia already was outnumbered almost 2 to 1 — but, ever the gambler, he now decided to dramatically increase the stakes in western Virginia. He would try again the maneuver that had brought him victory at Second Bull Run and at Chancellorsville. He would divide his forces in the face of the enemy and strike for his opponent's rear. On June 12, Lee sent for Jubal Early.

A few days before, Early had received promotion to the rank of lieutenant general and

had taken command of II Corps in place of the ailing Lieutenant General Richard S. Ewell. Now Lee told Early to take his corps west. Save Lynchburg and drive Hunter from the Valley, Lee said, and then, if Early thought it possible, go farther. Strike north, invade Maryland, drive toward Washington, D.C., and force the Federal government to loosen Grant's ever-tightening grip on Richmond and Petersburg.

Throughout the War, the Shenandoah Valley seemed to attract crusty characters; Jubal Early was a prime example. Like Grumble Jones, Early was another West Pointer who had quit the Army after a brief career to

Lieutenant General Jubal A. Early, ordered to defend Lynchburg, requisitioned with typical severity the rail cars needed to transport his army from Charlottesville. "Everything depends upon promptness, energy and dispatch," Early proclaimed. "I will hold all railroad agents and employees responsible with their lives for hearty cooperation with us."

return to his native southwest Virginia. He practiced law and rural politics in Rocky Mount and became notorious as a woman-hating bachelor with a coarse and unbridled tongue. Around an ever-present wad of chewing tobacco, Early expressed himself with a profanity so shocking and a sarcasm so biting that he could move men to laughter or outrage with equal facility — sometimes with the same remark.

Formidable in battle, contemptuous of his own appearance and dismissive of advice, Early had shared many characteristics with Jones. But in at least one respect they were very different: Early possessed a consuming ambition that drew him to those who could advance his career. Jubal Early never made the mistake of unleashing his tongue on a superior officer.

Major Henry Kyd Douglas, who had been on Stonewall Jackson's staff and was now Early's adjutant general, recalled Early's complexities: "Arbitrary, cynical, with strong prejudices, he was personally disagreeable; he made few admirers or friends either by his manners or his habits. If he had a tender feeling, he endeavored to conceal it and acted as though he would be ashamed to be detected in doing a kindness; yet many will recall little acts of General Early which prove that his heart was naturally full of loyalty and tenderness."

Neither Early nor his men were strangers to the Valley. His II Corps included the remnants of Stonewall Jackson's Army of the Shenandoah, which had bled off the strength of a Federal drive toward Richmond in 1862. Early had been a division commander under Ewell when II Corps took Winchester during Lee's drive toward Gettysburg in 1863. And the previous winter, Early had spent several months in the Valley in fruitless pursuit of William Averell's cavalry.

But there were deep shadows across his path now. Fearful attrition had reduced II Corps to 8,000 men — the size of a division. The proud Stonewall Brigade was now merely an understrength regiment. And hunger was a constant companion. For a year the standard daily ration had been a pint of cornmeal and a quarter pound of bacon per man. Many of the troops were barefoot, their clothing in tatters. But in the early hours of June 13 they willingly headed into the Valley to fight again, loping along at a pace of 20 miles a day.

Hunter, meanwhile, was pondering his next move from his headquarters at Staunton. Grant's orders had mentioned Charlottesville as a target, and he had sent with Sheridan a letter emphasizing that preference. But Hunter never received it. Now, at Strother's urging, Hunter chose a more ambitious prize — Lynchburg, a huge Confederate supply depot and a vital rail center linking Richmond with the West and the Deep South. He decided to continue up the Valley to Lexington, cut through the Blue Ridge at the Peaks of Otter and head east toward Lynchburg. "Unless Lee could detach a predominating force to drive us out," wrote Strother, "we would have our grip upon the vitals of the Confederacy."

It was a bold plan that required swift execution. But ammunition was scarce and Hunter had to send to Harpers Ferry for a fresh supply. Moreover, there were 1,000 stands of Confederate small arms to be destroyed along with the Staunton depot buildings and 50 miles of Virginia Central track. Thus it was not until June 10, five days after Piedmont and two days after Crook's arrival,

Vivid Sketches by a Soldier-Artist

A BUSHWHACKER

For Colonel David Hunter Strother *(right)*, chief of staff of the Federal army in the Shenandoah, the Civil War had interrupted a notable career as a writer and illustrator. Under the pseudonym *Porte Crayon* (Pencil Case), Strother had published several popular series of illustrated travel articles in *Harper's New Monthly Magazine*.

Although Shenandoah-born, Strother chose the Union side. He spent much of his military service in the Valley, where his artistic skill and knowledge of the terrain made him invaluable as a cartographer. When time allowed, he filled his own sketchbook; his gift for capturing both action and character resulted in some of the most vivid images of the campaign. A selection of engravings made from Strother's front-line sketches, with the artist's titles, is shown here.

DAVID HUNTER STROTHER

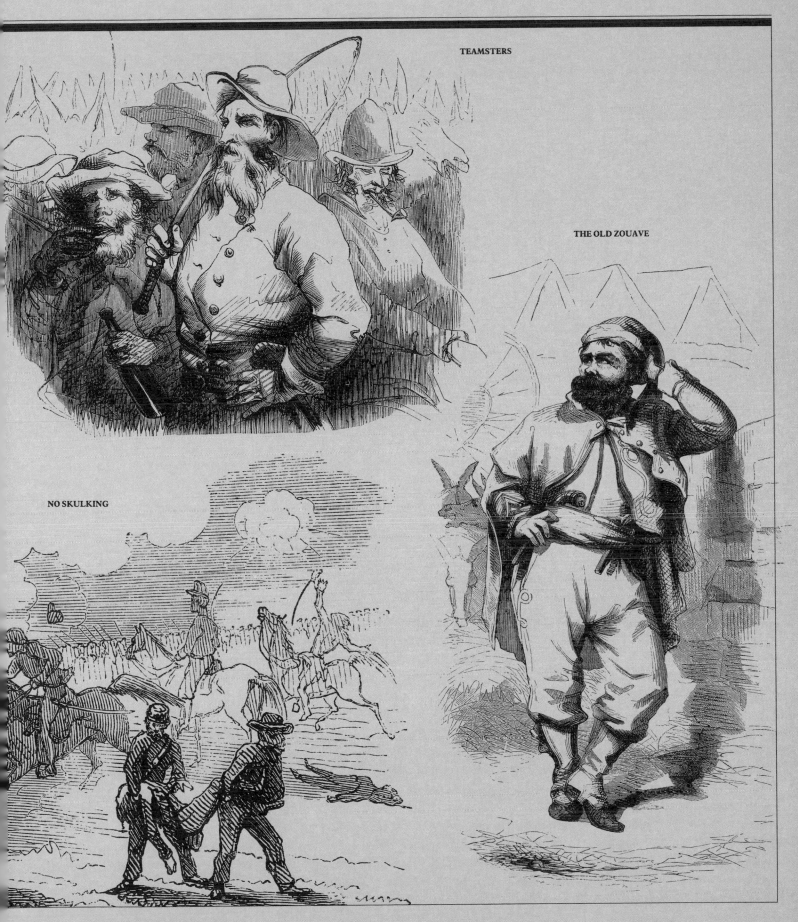

TEAMSTERS

THE OLD ZOUAVE

NO SKULKING

that Hunter's combined force, now styled the Army of West Virginia, was ready to march southward.

"Our route is through a most beautiful country," wrote Lieutenant Colonel Lincoln of the 34th Massachusetts, "extensive fields of luxuriant wheat bordering each side of the roads. Nothing but the gleaming lines of steel betray the presence of an armed body."

About noon the next day, Crook approached Lexington and the Virginia Military Institute, whose corps of cadets was again in the field. John McCausland's Confederate cavalrymen, who had been trying to slow Crook, had burned the bridge into the town. From a high cliff on the opposite side of the river, and from the nearby buildings of the institute, a few Confederate cannon and sharpshooters temporarily halted the powerful Federal force.

Averell took a brigade of cavalry across a ford south of Lexington to get behind the defenders. But the Federal horsemen moved slowly, and both McCausland's troopers and the VMI cadets escaped unscathed.

As the Federal troops marched through town on their way to the institute, two men of the 36th Ohio knocked on the door of a house and asked the owner for a drink of water. "I will give you a drink!" the man shouted. He seized a shotgun and fired it into the startled soldiers, killing one of them instantly. The others opened fire on the civilian and, as Private John Prather of the 91st Ohio recalled, "perforated his body with bullets until his skin looked more like a pepperbox than a human being."

By the time Hunter reached the VMI campus, the sacking had already begun. "We found soldiers, Negroes and riffraff disputing the plunder," Strother recalled. "The plunderers came out loaded with beds, carpets, cut velvet chairs, mathematical glasses and instruments, stuffed birds, charts, books, papers, arms, cadet uniforms and hats in the most ridiculous confusion."

Hunter had already made up his mind to torch the place, but before giving the order he asked his chief subordinates their opinion. Strother enthusiastically agreed, calling

With the ruins of VMI in the background, citizens go about their daily affairs on Lexington's main street after the Federal troops departed. During their three-day occupation, Union soldiers harvested acres of onions intended for the Confederate Army, burned a dozen storage barns, and slaughtered most of Lexington's cows and hogs for food.

the school "a tool of states rights conspirators" and "a most dangerous establishment where treason was systematically taught." There were military reasons, too, he argued: "The professors and cadets had taken the field against government troops, as an organized corps. The buildings had been used as a Rebel arsenal and fortress." DuPont took a more moderate stance; he favored burning the Barracks but saving the library and classrooms. Only Crook was totally opposed. "I did everything in my power to dissuade him," he recalled, "but all to no purpose."

Hunter made a point of telling Mrs. William Gilham, the daughter of a Federal officer and wife of a VMI professor who was off fighting with the Confederates, that her home would be among those set afire. "The house was a state building and it was fair to destroy it," Strother recorded. "Yet it was her only home, and it was hard to lose it. But she was a soldier's wife and a soldier's daughter so she set out some applejack, apologizing she had nothing better, and then went on to move out her furniture to the lawn." Strother had two army wagons transport Mrs. Gilham and her belongings to another house in town.

The next day, Hunter gave the order to burn the buildings and all the faculty houses except for the one belonging to VMI's superintendent, where Hunter had set up temporary headquarters. "I suppose he feels that the roof which has sheltered us should be saved," reckoned Strother, "whatever be its character."

The conflagration was spectacular, "A vast volume of black smoke rolled above the flames and covered half the horizon," Strother recalled. "The Institute burnt out about 2 p.m. and the arsenal blew up with a smart explosion. The General seemed to enjoy this scene."

While the fire raged, an officer brought Hunter a proclamation issued by the former Governor of Virginia, John Letcher of Lexington, calling on the people to wage guerrilla warfare "upon the vandal hordes of Yankee invaders." Incensed, Hunter ordered the absent Letcher's home burned, giving the family 10 minutes to clear out.

Nearby, a group of curious Federals had gathered at the grave of Stonewall Jackson in the Lexington town cemetery. The Confederate flag that flew beside the grave was torn down, and the staff was chopped up for souvenirs. One soldier scrawled in pencil on the general's marble headstone, "A good man and a brave soldier, but a traitor to God and his country."

Later that day Strother's attention was attracted to the bronze statue of George Washington that remained, unharmed by the flames, in front of VMI's gutted main building. It was a copy of the famous sculpture by the French artist Jean-Antoine Houdon, and Strother "felt indignant that this effigy should be left to adorn a country whose inhabitants were striving to destroy a government which he founded." Accordingly, the statue was crated and sent to Wheeling, West Virginia, as a trophy of war. Years later, when Strother became adjutant general of Virginia, he would arrange its return to a reconstructed VMI.

Duffié, meanwhile, had taken his cavalry division raiding across the Blue Ridge. He dodged the Confederate forces in Rockfish Gap above Waynesboro, skirmished with Mudwall Jackson's troopers, and destroyed a section of the railroad between Charlottesville and Lynchburg. It was a pointless expe-

dition — the railroad was immediately repaired by the Confederates. During this time Hunter got several reports that should have disposed him to make haste: He learned that Breckinridge and his division had joined Vaughn and Imboden in Rockfish Gap; that another Confederate force was heading west from Richmond; and that Sheridan had been driven back by Hampton. But it was June 13 before Duffié returned to Lexington; and the Federal army was not ready to resume its march to Lynchburg until the next day.

On June 15, in blistering heat and choking dust, the men labored over the Blue Ridge on a steep, tortuous track leading between the Peaks of Otter. "We have suffered much," wrote Lieutenant Colonel Lincoln. But, he added, "the scenery along the route is magnificent; mountain is piled high upon mountain. Far above our heads, we catch occasional glimpses of the moving column, the heavy rumbling of the artillery carriages coming to our ears like the low muttering of distant thunder; far below us we see the wagon train as it winds along its slow and heavy way." As the men descended, they plucked rhododendron blossoms and stuck them in the muzzles of their guns until, one officer recalled, the marching column looked like "a moving bank of flowers."

Strother claimed authorship of the plan to move against Lynchburg, but by June 16, with the army now east of the Blue Ridge and approaching the objective, he was suffering from misgivings. "I feel a vague uneasiness as to the result of our move," he wrote in his diary. "Lee will certainly relieve Lynchburg if he can. If he cannot, the Confederacy is gone up. If he does succeed in detaching a force, our situation is most hazardous."

Strother's worry was prophetic. On the day he wrote of his concern, General Breckinridge's 2,000 men marched into Lynchburg, which until that time had been virtually undefended. "Never were a lot of bronzed and dirty looking veterans, many of them barefooted, more heartily welcomed," a resident recalled. Breckinridge had left Rockfish Gap while Hunter was in Lexington and had marched 60 miles in the time it took the Federals to cover 35.

But the Confederate hold on Lynchburg was far from firm. For one thing, Imboden had let Breckinridge down. His men were still partisans at heart, it seemed, eager to defend their home counties but increasingly diffident the farther afield they traveled. Breckinridge had ordered Imboden to go after Duffié's cavalry on June 11: "Overtake, engage, and whip him." Three days later Breckinridge had sent the cavalryman after Hunter's forces: "Lose no time in finding their direction." On the 15th he was even more peremptory: "I want you to find his

position, and purposes, at all hazards." But by then Breckinridge had given up on Imboden. On the same day, he wired Richmond: "Enemy reported to be advancing, in force not known. The cavalry, under Imboden, doing less than nothing. If a good general officer cannot be sent at once for them, they will go to ruin."

To make matters worse, Breckinridge's men were exhausted from their forced march and Breckinridge himself was near collapse. At Cold Harbor his horse had been killed by an artillery round and had fallen on him, injuring his right leg. He was still unable to ride, and the exertions of getting his command to Lynchburg had left him bedridden, unable to oversee the preparations for the defense of the city.

Fortunately an old friend and experienced soldier, Major General Daniel Harvey Hill, happened to be in Lynchburg. Like Breckinridge, Hill had run afoul of Braxton Bragg while serving in the Army of Tennessee and still had not been given another command. Gratefully, Breckinridge accepted Hill's help in deploying the infantry — which once again included the VMI cadets — in the northern and western outskirts of the city. "There is no occasion for any disorder," Breckinridge reassured his men. "The enemy is advancing slowly. We will have General Early and large reinforcements tomorrow morning."

On June 17 fierce delaying actions by the Confederate cavalry slowed Hunter's advance to a crawl. Crook's infantry and Averell's cavalry were moving northeast on the Salem Pike, opposed at last by Imboden; a little farther out, Sullivan's division and Duffié's cavalry were coming in from the west, on the Forest road, against McCausland. Shortly after noon, Averell halted before a defensive line thrown up by Imboden at a Quaker meetinghouse five miles southwest of Lynchburg. About one hour later, General Early raced into the town from the northeast with one of his three divisions.

Hunter had ordered Crook and Averell not to attack until all the Federal forces were up. But Crook grew restive late in the afternoon and launched an unauthorized assault. "After waiting until nearly dark, I had to do all the work as it was," the disgusted Crook wrote later, "for I got no material assistance from anyone else."

While Crook's infantry advanced along the Salem Pike, the cavalry galloped to the east, around Imboden's left flank. Seeing that they were about to be enveloped, Imboden's troopers broke for the rear before contact was made, and the exultant Federals headed for the city.

They almost made it. But the aggressive Early, not content to await attack in Lynchburg, had ordered two of the brigades that had arrived with him from his former division — now commanded by Major General Stephen Dodson Ramseur — to push out along the Salem Pike. They had gone just two miles when they made contact with the Federal advance and were forced by heavy artillery fire to take cover.

The sun was setting by the time Hunter arrived on the scene, and he decided to halt operations for the night. He did so over the strenuous objections of his officers and men. "The curses that greeted this order were long and deep and loud," noted Private Prather of the 91st Ohio.

All night Crook's men listened in dismay to the sound of huffing locomotives pulling into Lynchburg and the cheering of relieved men greeting their reinforcements. But it was all a sham, staged by Early to disguise the fact that the rest of his corps had not arrived and that he was still outnumbered by more than 2 to 1. In the morning, he moved Breckinridge's division up to extend Ramseur's line northward, but it barely made a link with McCausland on the Forest road. The Lexington Turnpike farther north was completely undefended.

Hunter still was in no hurry. As daylight came and the hours passed on June 18, he ordered the enemy lines probed and deliberated on plans for an attack. Somehow he remained convinced that the taking of Lynchburg would be a simple matter.

While Duffié pushed McCausland closer to the city, Sullivan aligned his Federal division to the left of Crook's so that it straddled the Salem Pike with DuPont's artillery on the road in front of it. When Hunter and his staff rode forward to observe these preparations, Confederate artillery opened fire, narrowly missing the general's party with the initial salvo.

At length Hunter decided upon his tactics. He ordered Crook to move his infantry to the right, into some heavy woods, and make a flanking move on the enemy's position. It was about noon, and by then Jubal Early had grown tired of waiting.

"Some 15 or 20 minutes after Crook's division had disappeared in the timber," DuPont recalled, "the Confederates attacked us with great violence. Leaping over their defenses, the enemy's infantry, with terrific yells, assaulted the Union left and center, held respectively by Sullivan's division and the artillery brigade, my 26 remaining guns opening with a roar."

The Federals were unprepared for such

This filigree sword with scabbard was given to the recently promoted Brigadier General John McCausland by Lynchburg citizens for his role in defending the city in June 1864. A newspaper, soliciting public subscriptions to pay for the gift, suggested: "Let the individual contributions be small, so that all may contribute something to this memento of our gratitude."

audacity. "Before the desperate onset of the enemy, our lines seemed at first to recoil," wrote Major Harrison Pratt of the 34th Massachusetts. Hunter, badly shaken, quickly recalled Crook, who despite the confusion got his entire division turned around and back on the scene with what DuPont admiringly called "great promptitude."

Sullivan's men began to retreat, but Colonel Strother reported that Hunter "immediately faced them about and, waving his sword, led them back to their original position." They had been overwhelmed by the surprise attack, but "owing to the lionlike bearing of the commander, things were reinstated in a few minutes and the storm of musketry shook the earth."

"After swaying back and forth," wrote Major Pratt, "our entire line finally made a charge and drove the enemy into and over his first line of works." The fighting raged for an hour and a half, with Early persistently probing the Federal left, trying to drive a wedge between Sullivan's and Duffié's divisions. In response, Crook fed regiment after regiment of his division to the left to bolster Sullivan. "We are not whipped," wrote a soldier of the 34th Massachusetts. "In fact, we are holding our own, and a little more."

For a short time, according to Major Pratt's account, "the Stars and Stripes, borne by the color bearer of the 116th Ohio, were seen waving from the enemy's breastworks; but the word was given to withdraw, and soon our troops occupied nearly their former lines."

Hunter, who had progressed from gross underestimation to wild overestimation of the forces facing him, had decided to disengage. Upon confirming that he was indeed doing battle with Early's veteran II Corps, he assumed it to be a full 20,000 strong. In fact, even with the late afternoon arrival of the rest of Early's corps, the combined Confederate commands probably never equaled Hunter's. But the Federal leader was convinced, he said in his official report, that "the enemy had concentrated a force of at least double the numerical strength of mine."

Hunter added, "My troops had scarcely enough of ammunition left to sustain another well-contested battle" — an unlikely development after less than two hours of fighting. Hunter had suffered losses of 940 men in three days of combat and had probably inflicted 500 casualties on his opponents; he had simply lost heart.

The field quieted and evening came; that night it was the Confederates who listened anxiously to the sounds of enemy movements in the dark — presumably a shift toward the weaker defenses on the Confederate right. But the first light of day revealed to the defenders that the Federals were gone.

Demoralized, Hunter had abandoned the attack on Lynchburg, and was about to give up his hold on the Shenandoah Valley as well. He belatedly realized that by not going to Charlottesville first, as Grant had suggested, he had left in Confederate hands a railroad route that ran from Lynchburg north to Charlottesville and west into the Valley: Early could travel quickly by train to cut off a Federal retreat up the Shenandoah.

Thus when he reached Staunton, Hunter continued on into the Alleghenies, returning to the Kanawha Valley of West Virginia. In so doing he took himself and his army out of the War for a month and left wide open Jubal Early's road to Washington.

A Shield of Forts, a Surplus of Generals

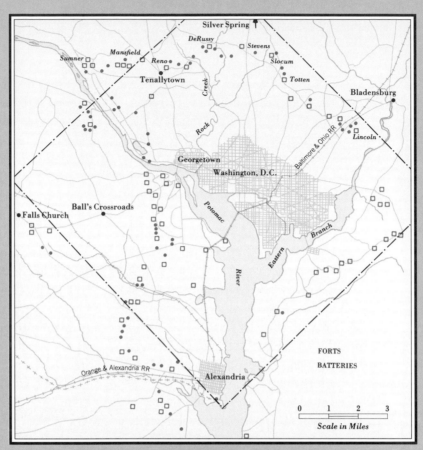

This map shows the ring of forts (*blue squares*) and batteries (*blue dots*) guarding Washington in the summer of 1864, including the critical line from Fort Lincoln to Fort Sumner north of the city. The forts formed a 37-mile perimeter around the city. The northernmost, Fort Stevens, sat only four miles from the White House.

The overall commander of Washington's northern defenses in 1864 was Major General Alexander McCook, shown below (*seated, center*) with his staff at a house near Fort Stevens. McCook tried desperately to sort out the leadership conflicts caused by too many generals (*opposite*) while keeping a watchful eye on Early's advance.

The last defense facing Jubal Early's bold Confederate drive to capture Washington in July 1864 was its ring of forts. But these defenses were badly flawed.

The forts themselves were not the problem. Fourteen wood-and-earth bastions formed a daunting wall north and west of the city, the area Early would certainly attack. The works were strongly built and heavily armed; Forts Totten and Slocum between them boasted 40 pieces of artillery. The forts' garrisons, however, had been dangerously thinned to provide reinforcements for Grant's army in Virginia. And a surplus of generals (*below*) shared authority over the forts, causing a confusion of command that threatened the effectiveness of the defensive system.

One of the officers jockeying for authority was Brigadier General Martin D. Hardin, who commanded the northwestern line of works extending from Fort DeRussy to Fort Sumner.

Adding to the confusion was Brigadier General Quincy A. Gillmore, needlessly summoned from New York by General Halleck to oversee the northeastern line from Fort Lincoln to Fort Totten.

Major General Christopher Augur, head of the Department of Washington, was superceded by McCook, but he clung to his command of XXII Corps, whose troops manned the capital's defenses.

Montgomery C. Meigs, although busy serving as the army's quartermaster general, also had a hand in Washington's defenses, commanding the line from Fort Totten to Fort DeRussy.

Despite the surfeit of commanders in Washington, Major General Horatio G. Wright's arrival in July of 1864 proved welcome: He brought badly needed reinforcements from his VI Corps.

Men of the 3rd Massachusetts Heavy Artillery stand at the entrance to Fort Totten (*inset*). Inside the fort (*below*), officers show off a rifled Parrott gun — on a carriage designed to absorb its recoil — that could hurl 100-pound shells six miles. If captured and turned, the gun could destroy the White House and the Capitol.

One-armed General Hardin (*seated, sixth from left*) and his staff escape the summer heat under an arbor inside Fort Slocum. By 1864 the larger forts had been in place for almost three years, giving the men time to add arbors and other amenities.

A view from a Fort Lincoln parapet shows storage buildings and bombproofs, as well as such armaments as siege howitzers and Parrott guns. The ornamental sentry box on the opposite rampart was probably built by soldiers seeking to fill off-duty hours.

Officers and men of Company F, 3rd Massachusetts Heavy Artillery, prepare for drill inside the northern rampart of Fort Stevens. Behind them a row of 30-pounder Parrott guns and 32-pounder Seacoast guns faces the field across which Jubal Early was hoping to advance. "The position was naturally strong," the Confederate general conceded in his memoirs. "Timber had been felled within cannon range all around and left on the ground, making a formidable obstacle, and every possible approach was raked by artillery."

PLAN.

A plan of Fort Stevens shows the disposition of its guns — including those shown opposite pointing north — as well as the placement of the powder magazines, blockhouse and bombproof. Like many of the Washington bastions, Fort Stevens took its name from a fallen hero of the Union Army: Brigadier General Isaac Stevens, a promising commander killed at Chantilly, Virginia, in 1862.

To the Gates of Washington

"We were all in high spirits and felt that we were about to enter the city with little or no opposition, where we would drag 'old Abe' out of hiding, and carry him in triumph off with us as a trophy to show our comrades."

PRIVATE ISAAC BRADWELL, 31ST GEORGIA WITH EARLY'S ARMY IN FRONT OF WASHINGTON

Jubal Early and his soldiers had grown callous to the destruction of war, yet they were shocked by what they saw as they marched into the Shenandoah behind David Hunter's retreating army. "Houses had been burned, and helpless women and children left without shelter," Early wrote later. "The country had been stripped of provisions and many families left without a morsel to eat. Furniture and bedding had been cut to pieces, and old men and women and children robbed of all the clothing they had except that on their backs." Weary and hungry themselves, the Confederates chased Hunter for three days. Then, seeing that the Federals were running for the Alleghenies, they broke off the pursuit and headed north down the Valley.

At Lexington the army passed the town's small cemetery. The officers dismounted and walked beside their horses; the men removed their hats and reversed their arms. A "hush as deep as midnight" fell over the thousands of men, according to one who was there, and the shrunken formations marched in solemn silence past Stonewall Jackson's grave.

"Not a man spoke, not a sound was uttered," Major Henry Kyd Douglas remembered, especially when Jackson's old division, including the depleted Stonewall Brigade, filed by. "Only the tramp, tramp of passing feet told that his surviving veterans were passing in review," wrote Douglas. "Alas, how few of them were left."

Arriving in Staunton on June 26, Early paused just long enough to realign his command before launching one of the most audacious gambles of the War: a surprise attack on Washington. "Jackson being dead," observed Douglas, "it is safe to say no other general in either army would have attempted it against such odds." Early counted 10,000 infantrymen in his four divisions, 4,000 cavalrymen in four brigades, and 40 guns. It was an emaciated little army; half of its infantrymen marched in worn-out shoes and many had none at all. But the men were experienced in combat, hardened to shortages and, above all, superbly led: Early's subordinates included not only the capable John Breckinridge and Robert Rodes, but two of the Confederacy's brightest young generals — John B. Gordon and Stephen Dodson Ramseur.

Major General Gordon was a lawyer, untrained in war but possessed of a natural aptitude for leading men in combat. With his fierce eyes, bristling goatee and graceful seat on a horse, the elegant 32-year-old Georgian looked every inch the military leader. The effect was not diminished by the deep scar on the left side of his face, the legacy of the last of five wounds he suffered on a single day at Antietam; one of his men called Gordon "most the prettiest thing you ever did see on a field of fight. It'ud put fight into a whipped chicken just to look at him."

An even faster rising star was that of Stephen Dodson Ramseur, who shortly after his 27th birthday had taken command of Early's old division. The youngest West Pointer

KENNEDY PALMER. Co.H.13TH VA.INFT.Vols
1861 To 1865 Aged 17. RICHMOND, VA.

A Confederate casualty of Jubal Early's surprise drive on Washington in July 1864, Private Kennedy Palmer of the 13th Virginia was severely wounded in skirmishing at Harpers Ferry. Palmer enlisted in 1861, at the age of 17; by the time he stood for this photograph — in his well-worn uniform and field gear — he was the picture of a seasoned campaigner.

(class of 1860) to make major general in the Confederate Army, Ramseur had grown a martial beard that added maturity to his boyish face. He had been wounded at Malvern Hill, Chancellorsville and Spotsylvania. But warfare had not yet quenched his youthful enthusiasm. "I have had three horses shot under me," he recounted in a letter to his bride of less than a year. "My saddle was shot through the pommel. I got four holes through my overcoat besides the ball which passed through my arm. I tell you these things, my Darling Wife, in order that you may be still more grateful to our Heavenly Father for his most wonderful and merciful preservation of my life."

While at Staunton, Early placed the divisions of Gordon and Brigadier General John Echols under Breckinridge. The divisions of Ramseur and Rodes — along with a new cavalry commander, Major General Robert Ransom Jr. — reported directly to Early. Thus organized, the army headed north again on June 28.

Jubal Early did not delude himself that he was about to win the War for the Confederacy. Indeed, he wrote years later that he was pursuing a "forlorn hope." The indefatigable Grant had side-stepped his entire army around Richmond and was besieging Petersburg. Sherman was driving into Georgia. With every passing day the Confederacy became smaller, its defenders fewer.

Still, the Federals had made no dramatic breakthroughs, and they had suffered grievous casualties. The Union's will to continue fighting was in question. It did not seem likely that Abraham Lincoln could retain the presidency in the fall elections, and his successor might well negotiate a peace that would leave the Confederacy intact. Thus the strategy now was to make the North ever more weary of the interminable War.

In the light of Black Dave Hunter's depredations, Early's soldiers had all the motivation they needed to march on Washington. "For the first time in the war," wrote Douglas, "I felt that vengeance ought not to be left entirely to the Lord."

By July 3, Early's army was approaching Martinsburg, where General Sigel with a small force was defending the northern end of the Valley. At the first whiff of danger, Sigel fell back across the Potomac and entrenched on Maryland Heights, opposite Harpers Ferry. The Federals burned the railroad and pontoon bridges behind them.

On July 5, after drawing supplies from Federal warehouses in Martinsburg, Early's men crossed the Potomac at Shepherdstown, and Gordon's division tried to bluff Sigel away from Maryland Heights. When the Federals resisted, Early decided not to press the issue. His intent was to march on Washington before Grant had time to react, leaving both Sigel and Hunter in his wake. He would worry about extricating himself later.

While the Confederate infantry marched eastward through Maryland on the morning of the 6th, Brigadier General John McCausland took his brigade of cavalry north to Hagerstown and threatened to burn the place unless paid a ransom. He collected $20,000 from the townspeople, the first reparation for Hunter's destruction of private property in the Shenandoah.

Soldiers escorting a Confederate supply train take their ease as the ponderous wagons labor through the Shenandoah Valley. Such movements were agonizing, especially in the stifling summer heat: "We would march two miles and rest ten minutes," reported a private in Early's army.

General Grant was slow to believe that Early would dare to cross the Potomac. But because the civilians and politicians of Washington, Maryland and Pennsylvania were about to raise a fearful uproar, Grant reluctantly detached a division from the Army of the Potomac's VI Corps as well as 3,000 dismounted cavalrymen and sent them to protect Washington.

The reinforcements had a long way to travel. In the meantime, the defense of most of the state of Maryland was the responsibility of Major General Lew Wallace, another lawyer who had shown some aptitude for leading men in combat. A lean, sharp-featured man with soulful eyes, Wallace's most enduring fame would come later as the author of the novel *Ben Hur: A Tale of the Christ*. His military career had foundered at the Battle of Shiloh in 1862 when his division took a wrong road and failed to arrive in time for the first day's fighting. For almost two years thereafter, Wallace had received only insignificant assignments. Then, in March of 1864 President Lincoln had given Wallace command of the Middle Department, with headquarters in Baltimore.

Wallace got the first hint of danger from the west from John W. Garrett, president of the B & O Railroad. Garrett called at Wallace's headquarters on July 2 to express concern about reports from his railroad agents near Harpers Ferry that large numbers of Confederate troops were approaching. Wallace immediately saw the prospect of another Confederate invasion of the North and dispatched Brigadier General Erastus B. Tyler's brigade of Baltimore militia westward to meet the threat. And in the early-morning hours of July 5, while Early was crossing the Potomac River, Wallace rushed by train to the western boundary of his department — the Monocacy River.

The railroad crossed the Monocacy 45 miles west of Baltimore and three miles southeast of the little city of Frederick, Maryland. Major roads led from Frederick to both Baltimore and Washington, and Wallace concluded that whichever city the Confederates intended to strike, they would have to cross the Monocacy at this junction.

Two miles upriver, north of the massive iron railroad bridge, was a stone bridge boasting an eight-foot-high, vaselike edifice for which the structure was nicknamed the Jug Bridge. This span carried the Baltimore pike across the river. Three hundred yards south of the railroad, the Georgetown Turnpike to Washington crossed the Monocacy via a covered wooden bridge.

During the next two days Wallace gathered at the Monocacy about 2,500 defenders and Captain Frederic W. Alexander's Baltimore battery of six guns. It was a wobbly force of militiamen and home guards until, by a stroke of good fortune, Wallace was able to add to it 230 troopers from the veteran 8th Illinois Cavalry who had been patrolling at Point of Rocks, near the confluence of the Monocacy and Potomac Rivers. Wallace desperately needed cavalry to locate his enemy, and Lieutenant Colonel David R. Clendenin responded immediately to the urgent summons — even though he was not under Wallace's command.

The horsemen reached Frederick late on July 6, then at daybreak they headed west to find the Confederates. In Catoctin Pass, about five miles from town, they encountered and drove off a detachment of enemy riders. But once on the other side of the pass, they found serious trouble.

The order below, signed by Brigadier General John McCausland (*right*), itemizes Confederate demands on the citizens of Hagerstown, Maryland, to avert the burning of their town. Three banks raised the $20,000 cash ransom, but the demand for clothing sufficient for 1,500 men was not met.

Clendenin's men spotted four regiments of Virginia cavalry fanning out on either side of the road ahead. It was Brigadier General Bradley T. Johnson's 800-man brigade, screening the advance of Early's main body.

Outflanked and outnumbered, the Federals fell back into the pass. Clendenin saw that he could not hold and sent a rider across the river to warn Wallace that the Confederates would be in Frederick within hours. By mid-afternoon the tired Federal troopers were driven back to the town's outskirts, where Wallace had deployed a regiment of Maryland militia, a small force of cavalry and three of Alexander's guns. Johnson—a native of Frederick, fighting now to capture his hometown—made his first charge on the thin Union line at 4 p.m. Encouraged by the example of the stalwart 8th Illinois, the inexperienced Federals stood fast. After two hours of sparring, the Federals counterattacked and forced the Confederates to fall back to the Catoctin Pass.

Shortly after dawn on July 8, Wallace was cheered by the arrival of the first reinforcements from the Army of the Potomac. The 10th Vermont, part of VI Corps's 3rd Division under Brigadier General James B. Ricketts, was coming into Baltimore by steamer and was proceeding to Monocacy by rail. By now even Grant was alarmed; he had ordered the rest of VI Corps — and two XIX Corps divisions that were beginning to arrive at Fort Monroe by sea from Louisiana — to head for Washington.

Wallace still had no idea of the size or the intent of the approaching Confederates. He posted the new men in Frederick, placing the entire command under Tyler. Throughout the day, the remainder of Colonel William Truex's VI Corps brigade continued to come in by train.

A Confederate infantry column was rumored to be moving toward Urbana, southeast of Frederick, and Wallace concluded that the raiders must be headed for Washington. His makeshift army "was probably too small to defeat them, but certainly strong enough to gain time," Wallace wrote later. "I made up my mind to fight."

That night, Wallace pulled all but a few skirmishers out of Frederick and deployed most of his forces on the eastern bank of the Monocacy, where he had the advantages of high ground, the river in his front and good roads behind him on which to make the inevitable retreat. He had by now received the last of his reinforcements, five regiments of Colonel Matthew R. McClennan's two brigades of Ricketts' division.

General Tyler's militia held the Federal right, a two-mile stretch from the railroad north to the Jug Bridge. A detachment of skirmishers held the bridgehead across the river on the Baltimore pike. Wallace, expecting the main Confederate thrust to be toward Washington, deployed Ricketts' veterans across the Georgetown pike and along a low ridge that extended south from the river to an estate called Araby, with an imposing red-brick manor house, owned by the Kieffer Thomas family. Ricketts also posted men on the west bank of the river to defend the railroad bridge and the covered bridge for as long as they could.

It was four in the morning before the Federal dispositions were complete. Then, as the fierce sun rose and the heat regained its grip on the countryside, the waiting began. Six thousand worried men scanned the sky to the west, where dust clouds raised by the approaching Confederates were gathering. "We were much depressed," said a soldier of the 10th Vermont, "for we knew we were greatly outnumbered."

Jubal Early was still not sure what awaited him along the Monocacy on the morning of July 9. He could see that it was a sizable Federal force, and although Johnson had reported that the troops were raw militia and not a serious threat, Early could not afford to make a mistake deep in enemy territory. His approach was cautious. He ordered McCausland's cavalry to move south to sever the railroad and telegraph lines to Washington; then McCausland was to cross the river and if at all possible seize the railroad bridge at Monocacy Junction.

Meanwhile, Johnson was to take his cavalry around Frederick to the north, cut the railroads to Baltimore, threaten that city and hold himself ready to undertake a possible secondary mission: releasing the 17,000 Confederates being held at Point Lookout, 70 miles southeast of Washington. General Lee, in his anguish over the dwindling size of his army, had become enthralled with the idea of freeing the prisoners, and he had encouraged Early to accomplish it somehow.

Ramseur's division quickly drove the Federal skirmishers out of Frederick and headed southeast along the Georgetown pike while Rodes took his men east on the Baltimore pike. Early kept Breckinridge's two divisions with him near Frederick and waited to see what developed.

The debt incurred by General Hunter was never far from Early's mind; when he reached Frederick at 8 a.m., the Confederate commander informed the mayor that the citizens must hand over $200,000 (McCausland had settled for 10 percent of that amount at Hagerstown) or see their town burned. The residents begged for time to raise the cash—and, no doubt, to see how the impending battle came out. Early gave them a few hours.

At midmorning Rodes encountered Tyler's entrenched skirmishers, six companies of the 149th Ohio, two miles southeast of Frederick in front of the Jug Bridge. And Ramseur came up against the similarly thin line across the road Early really wanted—the Georgetown pike to Washington—more than two miles to the southeast. Rodes and Ramseur formed lines of battle and began to test the Federals' strength with skirmishers and artillery.

About 200 men of the 1st Maryland Potomac Home Brigade held a portion of the line that included a log blockhouse guarding the approaches to the B & O bridge and the nearby covered bridge. The Marylanders were joined by a company of the 9th New York Heavy Artillery and by 75 men of the veteran 10th Vermont. George E. Davis, first lieutenant of the Vermonters, was in command; he placed most of his skirmishers behind

Major General Lew Wallace commanded the improvised army that bought precious time for the defense of Washington with its stand at the Monocacy River. Years later, when Wallace met General John Gordon, who had opposed him there, Gordon saluted Wallace as the only man who had "whipped" him in the War: "You snatched Washington out of our hands — there was the defeat."

the railroad cut at the entrance to the bridges. His roughly triangular defense was covered by a 24-pounder howitzer mounted across the river on the bluff overlooking the bridges. The position was a strong one and the men had been ordered to "hold the bridges at all hazards."

Confederates of Colonel Charles C. Blacknall's 23rd North Carolina, from Brigadier General Robert D. Johnston's brigade, rushed the blockhouse, which was the key to the Federal defense. They pushed to within 20 feet of the structure before point-blank fire drove the survivors back. Colonel Blacknall narrowly escaped death as a bullet glanced off his head, leaving him unconscious but alive. His men carried him to the rear as they retreated.

The respite for the Federals was brief. Brigadier General Armistead L. Long, Early's chief of artillery, soon brought 16 guns to

Jubal demanding Earley Tribute

4 inches

Jubal Early, on horseback, demands $200,000 in greenbacks from the city fathers of Frederick, Maryland, in this pen-and-ink sketch by Charles W. Reed, a Union soldier. Reed, who was not present, erred in at least one detail: The weather that July 9 was not rainy but blistering hot and dry.

bear on the Federals east of the river. The six Parrott rifles of Alexander's battery, though severely outgunned, managed temporarily to keep the Confederates at bay. Early now realized he was facing more than militia. "The enemy's position was too strong, and the difficulties of crossing the Monocacy under fire too great, to attack in front without greater loss than I was willing to incur," he wrote later. He rode south along the river instead, downstream from the Georgetown pike bridge, seeking a way to get across the Monocacy and at the Federal left.

He spotted McCausland's cavalry, intent on its second assignment — taking the bridges if possible. McCausland's troopers found the ford for which Early had been searching. They splashed across the river, drove away Company B of the ubiquitous 8th Illinois Cavalry and cantered into the yard of the Worthington family farm, which occu-

pied the northern end of Brooks' Hill, a ridge overlooking Ricketts' line. From there they could see the blueclad ranks on either side of the Thomas house, and beyond them, the road to Washington. Presuming the enemy to be only militia, McCausland had his men dismount, send their horses to the rear and advance through a field of waist-high corn.

General Wallace saw all this from his command post on a hill overlooking the railroad and the covered highway bridge. He sat his horse, listening and watching. In response to the threat to his left, Wallace ordered the covered bridge burned to keep Ramseur's men on the other side of the river. Then he instructed Ricketts to change front to the southwest and face McCausland instead of Ramseur. Colonel McClennan's five regiments held Ricketts' right, Colonel Truex's five the left. Their shift was made difficult by the enfilade fire of a section of Captain John

The Invalids' Call to Arms

In the patchwork of Federal units pressed into service to defend Washington's northern perimeter as Early's army approached were seven regiments of the Veteran Reserve Corps. Originally called the Invalid Corps, the VRC had been organized to offer light-duty status to men whose wounds made them unfit for field service, thereby releasing able-bodied men for combat.

The men of the VRC were grouped according to their degree of disability. Those in the 1st Battalion, infirm but not maimed, were armed with muskets and performed garrison and escort duties; the 2nd Battalion, amputees, carried revolvers and lightweight swords and served as nurses and clerks. This composition, while useful, fostered little esprit de corps. The men were further set apart by their distinctive uniform (below), which some thought stigmatized them as shirkers. Responding to the threat against Washington, the invalids got a rare taste of glory.

A sergeant of the VRC stands at attention; his cap pouch and cartridge belt identify him as a member of the musket-bearing 1st Battalion. The uniform jacket (below), unlike that worn by the rest of the army, was sky blue, matching the trousers.

Camp Fry, the barracks housing two of the 14 VRC regiments garrisoning Washington, stretches from the statue of George Washington at Washington Circle south toward the Potomac River. The camp was named for Colonel James Fry, the first U.S. provost marshal general, who dealt with draftees, recruits, deserters and the corps of wounded veterans.

L. Massie's Virginia artillery, on a hill less than 800 yards away.

Barely in time, one of Truex's regiments, the 87th Pennsylvania, got into position behind a fence dividing the Thomas and Worthington farms and lay down, out of sight of the advancing Virginians. Without their horse-holders, the Confederates were only about 700 strong—and they were advancing against three times their number. A Federal soldier would remember the dismounted troopers approaching "in perfect order, all the while shouting their ominous, defiant battle cry."

Suddenly the fence came alive as the Federals leaped to their feet and fired a murderous volley into the astonished Virginians, whose battle line all but disappeared. The rows of corn sheltered from sight not only the dead and wounded but crouched, running men as well. Shouting that they had been led into an ambush, the survivors reeled back through the Worthington yard and kept going until they reached the edge of the river.

It took almost two hours to re-form the line, but at 2 p.m., incredibly, the Virginians attacked again. This time they veered to the right, keeping cover between themselves and the deadly fence, feeling for the Federal flank. In response, the 87th Pennsylvania began extending to the left on the run, trying to stay between the enemy and the Georgetown Turnpike; but the Federal line began to bend back toward the yard of the Thomas house. Running, loading and firing in the stifling heat, the Virginians pushed the thinned-out Federals from the Thomas house and clung there, on a slight rise of ground, under heavy fire.

Wallace ordered the 87th Pennsylvania and another regiment, the 14th New Jersey, to charge across the fields and retake the Thomas house. Just as the Federals began to move, recalled Major Peter Vredenburgh of the 14th, "the Rebels came in force from behind the house. They advanced over the crest on a line with the house before the firing became brisk, and then it opened as severely as I have ever heard from such a small force." The Federals also came under bombardment from the Confederate batteries across the river but, Vredenburgh wrote, "our boys fought as if they were fighting for their own homes, and literally mowed down the first two lines of Rebels. Our men at Thomas' gate then charged up his yard and across his field right up to his house, and drove the enemy around the corners, behind the barn." McCausland at last realized the precariousness of his position and pulled his troops back.

General Early had ordered Breckinridge to move Gordon's division across the river where the cavalry had crossed and launch a flank attack to drive Wallace from his position. By the time Gordon could get his men in place it was midafternoon, and Gordon found himself facing a confident enemy posted behind cover on high ground. His support, General Echols' division, was marching from Frederick but would not be up for some time. Worse, Gordon's men must advance over fields laced with stout fences and, on the Thomas farm, studded with large shocks of grain.

Nevertheless, Gordon ordered an assault in echelon, with each brigade following the one to its right into action. Brigadier General Clement A. Evans' Georgians would be in the lead; Brigadier General Zebulon York would commit his Louisiana brigade next;

Major General Stephen D. Ramseur won Early's admiration for the way his "courage and energy seemed to gain new strength in the midst of confusion and disorder." Ramseur's wartime bride, Nellie (*right*), was his first cousin and the daughter of a wealthy North Carolina planter. During the summer of 1864, she was awaiting the birth of their first child.

sion was in place in front of Gordon, but it was overextended and in the air on the left. To the north, Tyler's men still held the Jug Bridge, although they were being pressed hard by Rodes.

Wallace had decided that "it was time to get away." But he could not safely disengage in the face of an attack, and now Evans' Georgia brigade came into view, crossing the fence on the crest of Brooks' Hill and charging the left of Truex's line. As the Federal skirmishers fell back, one of them fired from the dubious cover of a shock of wheat into the oncoming ranks of the 26th Georgia — and died with 18 bullets in his body. Then the Georgians came to the second of the many obstacles in their way — a high, stout rail fence more than 100 yards from the Federal line.

As the attackers clambered over this fence, Gordon wrote later, "they were met by a tempest of bullets." General Evans was struck down with a Minié ball in his side, and command of the brigade passed to Colonel E. M. Atkinson of the 26th Georgia.

Private Peter Robertson of the 106th New York, in Truex's brigade, recalled, "Such a fire was kept up that no mortal foe could cross that field." Yet cross it they did. With the shocks of wheat preventing them from closing their ranks or returning fire effectively, and with their comrades dropping around them with fearful frequency, the Georgians pressed on.

Major Edwin Dillingham of the 10th Vermont stood in the partial cover of the Worthington's sunken access road, one of his men recalled, "swinging his saber and yelling, 'Give it to them boys! We have them on the flank! Pitch it into them! This is fun!'"

The Confederate advance became disor-

and Brigadier General William Terry's Virginians would follow York's troops in reserve. Gordon hoped to overlap the Federal left and roll it up toward the river with sequential thrusts.

About 3 p.m., while Gordon's division formed for the attack, General Wallace assessed the Federal situation. Ricketts' divi-

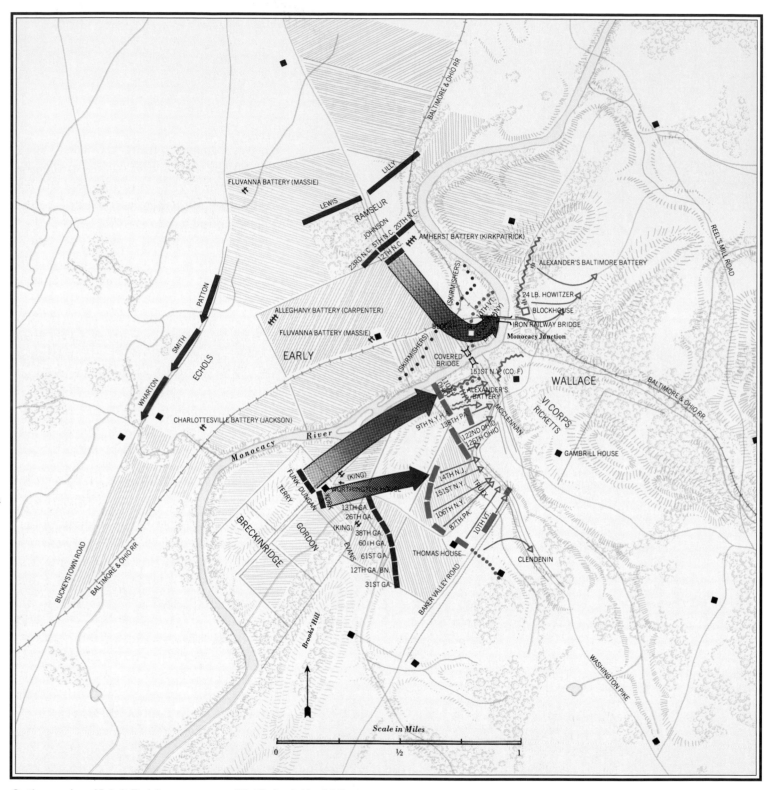

FLUVANNA BATTERY (MASSIE)

LEWIS

LILLY

RAMSEUR

JOHNSON

23RD N.C. 5TH N.C. 20TH N.C.

12TH N.C.

AMHERST BATTERY (KIRKPATRICK)

BALTIMORE & OHIO RR

REEL'S MILL ROAD

(SKIRMISHERS)

ALEXANDER'S BALTIMORE BATTERY

PATTON

SMITH

ECHOLS

WHARTON

ALLEGHANY BATTERY (CARPENTER)

FLUVANNA BATTERY (MASSIE)

EARLY

24 LB. HOWITZER

BLOCKHOUSE

IRON RAILWAY BRIDGE

Monocacy Junction

(SKIRMISHERS)

COVERED BRIDGE

151ST N.Y. (CO. F)

WALLACE

CHARLOTTESVILLE BATTERY (JACKSON)

River

Monocacy

9TH N.Y. H.

138TH PA.

ALEXANDER'S BATTERY

McCLENNAN

VI CORPS

RICKETTS

BALTIMORE & OHIO RR

122ND OHIO

126TH OHIO

Gambrill House

FUNK DUNGAN

(KING)

14TH N.J.

151ST N.Y.

TRUX

TERRY

BRECKINRIDGE

GORDON

13TH GA.

26TH GA.

(KING)

38TH GA.

106TH N.Y.

87TH PA.

EVANS

60TH GA.

61ST GA.

12TH GA. BN.

31ST GA.

10TH VT.

THOMAS HOUSE

Thomas House

CLENDENIN

BUCKEYSTOWN ROAD

BALTIMORE & OHIO RR

BAKER VALLEY ROAD

WASHINGTON PIKE

Brooks' Hill

Scale in Miles

0   ½   1

On the morning of July 9, Early's Confederate army faced Wallace's outnumbered Federals entrenched behind the Monocacy River, blocking Early's advance on Washington. At noon, as Rodes threatened the Federal right (*not shown*) and Ramseur pressed the Federal skirmish line defending Monocacy Junction, Gordon's division crossed the river and attacked the Union left. Gordon's onslaught drove back Ricketts' division of VI Corps, forcing Wallace to retreat toward Baltimore.

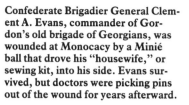
Confederate Brigadier General Clement A. Evans, commander of Gordon's old brigade of Georgians, was wounded at Monocacy by a Minié ball that drove his "housewife," or sewing kit, into his side. Evans survived, but doctors were picking pins out of the wound for years afterward.

ganized; little semblance remained of brigade or regimental battle lines. One regiment, the 61st Georgia, suffered heavily from the fire of Federal sharpshooters concealed in the Thomas house. The 61st's colonel, J. H. Lamar, was shot off his horse as he rode at the head of his men and his second-in-command, Lieutenant Colonel J. D. Van Valkenburg, was killed as well. Captain B. S. Boatright of the 12th Georgia Battalion, also with Evans' brigade, recalled that he had only four men with him as he entered the Thomas yard. A sudden volley from behind the embankment of the Georgetown pike cut down all four of Boatright's companions and sent a ball through his coat sleeve.

The Georgians at last came to a standstill and General Gordon sent a message to Breckinridge, who was back at the Worthington house, asking that reinforcements be sent up. Fortunately for the Confederates, several guns from Major William McLaughlin's artillery battalion had been sent across the river already. Lieutenant Colonel J. Floyd King, second-in-command of Early's artillery, had quickly positioned them on high ground overlooking the Federal line. One of the guns opened fire on the Thomas house, sending shot and shells crashing through its brick walls and dislodging the Federal riflemen there.

Now General York brought his Louisianians into action to the left of Evans' brigade. He deployed his men from column into line of battle in the face of the enemy and dashed forward, clearing the Worthington cornfield of Federal skirmishers. They drove Ricketts' men from their front, then rushed ahead and slammed into the 14th New Jersey. That regiment had already lost its commanding officer and his successor to the fire of Evans' Georgians. In the renewed attack, more than 140 Federal soldiers were shot down. The 14th's line sagged in the center but held; the attack rolled on into the Ohio regiments of the second Federal line.

Ricketts had rushed so many of his men to bolster the hard-pressed Federal left that his right was no longer anchored on the river. This was precisely what Gordon had hoped his attack would achieve, and he lost no time sending Terry's Virginia brigade to thrust at Ricketts' right flank.

Just as Gordon's Confederates began their drive against Ricketts' right, the situation for the Federal skirmishers across the Monocacy reached a crisis point. The men had successfully withstood a Confederate attempt to cut them off from the railroad bridge; but as pressure mounted, the Maryland militiamen melted away across the bridge. Lieutenant Davis and his handful of Vermonters now faced an entire Confederate division alone. When Gordon's attack

reached its peak, the 12th North Carolina charged the blockhouse. As the attackers surged forward, Davis could see the beginning of a Federal retreat across the river. "The division headquarters flag was crossing the track in our rear," he reported. "We must leave now or never." Davis ordered his men to cross the bridge.

The retreating soldiers had to hop from tie to tie, exposed to enemy rifle fire. "It seemed ages before we reached the other side," Davis wrote later, "though in reality it must have been only a few minutes. One poor fellow fell through the bridge to the river, 40 feet below, and several were taken prisoners,

for the enemy had been close at our heels all the way." But most of the Vermonters escaped to rejoin their regiment, and Lieutenant Davis was later awarded the Congressional Medal of Honor.

Swarming Confederates soon drove the Federal skirmishers from the western end of the ridge that ran parallel to the Monocacy. General Terry sent Colonel J. H. Funk's Consolidated Regiment—fragments of the old Stonewall Brigade—advancing to the left down the riverbank. Funk's Virginians were hidden from the Federals by the ridge until they opened fire at close range against the 110th Ohio, which was sheltering in the

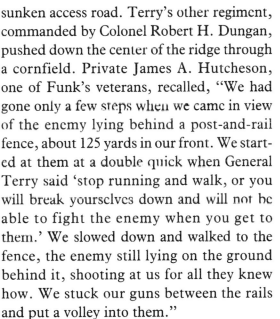
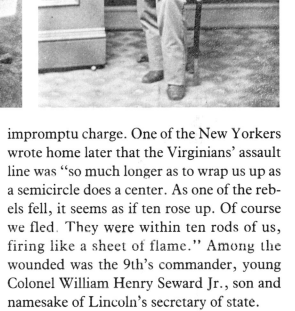

Among the 1,294 Union casualties at Monocacy were these three members of James Ricketts' division, which took the brunt of the Confederates' climactic charge. Lieutenant Colonel Edward P. Taft (*left*) of the 9th New York Heavy Artillery suffered a leg wound that led to his death two and a half years later. Private John Free (*center*) of the 110th Ohio and Captain Symmes H. Stults (*right*) of the 14th New Jersey were killed outright.

sunken access road. Terry's other regiment, commanded by Colonel Robert H. Dungan, pushed down the center of the ridge through a cornfield. Private James A. Hutcheson, one of Funk's veterans, recalled, "We had gone only a few steps when we came in view of the enemy lying behind a post-and-rail fence, about 125 yards in our front. We started at them at a double quick when General Terry said 'stop running and walk, or you will break yourselves down and will not be able to fight the enemy when you get to them.' We slowed down and walked to the fence, the enemy still lying on the ground behind it, shooting at us for all they knew how. We stuck our guns between the rails and put a volley into them."

By this time Terry's Confederates had brought Ricketts' right flank under a galling enfilade fire that even the VI Corps veterans could not withstand for long. The Federals fell back down the hill toward the Georgetown pike, but not before inflicting 59 casualties on Dungan's regiment alone.

Terry's men re-formed and pushed farther along the river. The 110th Ohio and the 9th New York Heavy Artillery, in line as infantry near the river, caught the worst of the

impromptu charge. One of the New Yorkers wrote home later that the Virginians' assault line was "so much longer as to wrap us up as a semicircle does a center. As one of the rebels fell, it seems as if ten rose up. Of course we fled. They were within ten rods of us, firing like a sheet of flame." Among the wounded was the 9th's commander, young Colonel William Henry Seward Jr., son and namesake of Lincoln's secretary of state.

Ricketts' right was caving in, and he began a difficult disengagement under fire. Thanks to the discipline of the VI Corps veterans, he was able to make a retrograde movement that was just measurably slower than a rout, along the river to the Baltimore pike. Tyler's militiamen held the Jug Bridge long enough for the remaining Federals to get past and away; by the time the firing sputtered to a stop, it was too late in the day for Early to push on. There were dead to bury, wounded to tend and scattered units to pull together. And there was the matter of that $200,000 ransom, which the city fathers of Frederick now handed over. The march to Washington would have to be postponed until the next morning, July 10.

Wallace headed for Baltimore, having garnered 24 precious hours for the lashing together of a defense of the Federal capital. He had paid a price of 1,294 casualties. Confederate losses probably numbered close to 700 — men Early could not replace.

Wallace's achievement in defeat was not appreciated at first; he was relieved temporarily as Middle Department commander, but he was soon restored to the post by General Grant, who eventually concluded that Wallace had contributed more to the Federal cause by losing at Monocacy "than often falls to the lot of a commander of equal force to render by means of a victory."

Refugees fleeing before Early's advance infected the citizens of Washington and Baltimore with wild rumors about Confederate numbers and atrocities. Officials representing the capital's myriad civilian agencies and military commands were galvanized into frenzied activity. They dredged the hospitals and assembled squads of the walking wounded, gathered improvised units of government employees and marched them to the city's defenses, and prepared the Potomac River bridges for demolition.

Chief of staff Halleck seethed at the confusion. When he received an offer of help from yet another general, this one in far-off New York City, Halleck sent a scathing reply: "We have five times as many generals here as we want, but are greatly in need of privates. Anyone volunteering in that capacity will be thankfully received."

President Lincoln and General Grant took a more sanguine view of the threat. The city was surrounded by a formidable ring of defenses bristling with more than 900 cannon and mortars. Fewer than 10,000 troops could be assembled on the morning of July 11, but 15,000 men from VI Corps and XIX Corps were on the way. "Let us be vigilant," Lincoln wired a group of Baltimore citizens, "but keep cool."

Coolness was in short supply as the inexperienced gunners and citizen-soldiers on Washington's northern ramparts awaited the approaching enemy. At Rockville, the Confederate infantry turned east to Silver Spring and then south along the Seventh Street road. There, at midday, Jubal Early surveyed Fort Stevens, the northernmost of Washington's defensive works, while his cavalry fanned out to probe the Federal line to the left and right.

Early's first look at Fort Stevens told him that there was still a chance to break through. "The works were but feebly manned," he wrote later. Beyond them, Early could see the dome of the U.S. Capitol, five miles away, shimmering in the July heat. Early ordered General Rodes, whose division was in the lead, to form a line of battle "as rapidly as possible, throw out skirmishers, and move into the works."

But the tantalizing prize was beyond reach. The Confederate soldiers were willing enough, but after a day of fighting, another day of hard marching in enervating heat, and a night so hot and humid that rest was impossible, they had been exhausted when they began that morning's march. They had fallen out by the hundreds, and those who were present to receive Early's orders were too weak to do more than spar with the Federal skirmishers. Precious hours slipped from the fuming Early's grasp, and a Federal officer wrote later, "It was a fatal pause."

By midafternoon, the first detachment of VI Corps reached the defensive line. The troops had disembarked from their steamers

A Great Escape That Failed

One of the most ambitious missions of the War fell to Brigadier General Bradley T. Johnson, who commanded a cavalry brigade in the Confederate army Jubal Early was leading toward Washington in July of 1864. Johnson's daunting task: to ride with his men 300 miles in four days and liberate 17,000 Confederates being held in the Federal prison camp at Point Lookout, Maryland.

Johnson's circuitous route would take him north of Baltimore, then south past Washington — wrecking railroad track and telegraph lines as he went — and finally down the Maryland peninsula to its remote tip. With the help of a Confederate gunboat that was somehow to penetrate the Federal blockade of Southern ports, he was to free the prisoners and march them to Washington, arming them at the Federal arsenals that Early hoped to capture.

The dubious scheme quickly foundered. The Federals got word of the plan from a Confederate deserter and reacted swiftly, alerting the guards at Point Lookout and doubling the seagoing watch at the prison to four armed craft. These defenses were not tested. When Early's march stalled on the outskirts of Washington, he summoned Johnson, who was still many miles from his objective, to join in the Confederate retreat.

Bradley T. Johnson, a native of Maryland, was selected to rescue the Confederate prisoners at Point Lookout in July 1864. He had been promoted to brigadier general only a few days earlier.

The Federal complex at Point Lookout, where the Potomac River flows into the Chesapeake Bay, included a hospital (*lower left*), stockades for prisoners (*upper right*) and a beachfront command center (*inset*).

at the Sixth Street wharves and had immediately fallen prey to the confusion that gripped the capital. With their corps commander, Major General Horatio G. Wright, at their head, the men had marched toward Georgetown until staff officers sent by Halleck got them stopped and headed north up Seventh Street toward the enemy. Amid the shouting, marching and clatter, one figure was notable for his calm — President Lincoln gnawed imperturbably on a piece of hardtack as he watched the arrival of the troops sent to save his capital.

The reinforcements were merely the first of many. With their coming, as Lincoln knew, there was no longer any possibility of the loss of Washington. The Federal objective now was offensive, not defensive: Catch Early and punish him so severely that Confederates would never again think of pushing across the Potomac.

Early and his four division commanders met that night in a Silver Spring mansion owned by the absent Francis P. Blair, a close adviser to President Lincoln. The Confederate officers helped themselves to the Blair wine cellar and talked about launching an assault on the city's works in the morning. They joked about escorting Breckinridge to his former place as presiding officer of the U.S. Senate, but they conceded that their time was running out.

During the night, Early learned that troops from two Federal corps were streaming into Washington from Virginia. That meant he had accomplished a major objective of his raid — and that he was in increasing danger of being overwhelmed. At first light, Early surveyed his situation; as expected, the faded blue uniforms of seasoned troops filled the Federal lines. "I had, therefore, reluctantly to give up all hopes of capturing Washington, after I had arrived in sight of the dome of the Capitol," he wrote. The Confederates would stay that day, July 12, menacing and skirmishing. But there would be no general assault, and that night they would head back to Virginia. Bradley Johnson, who was pressing toward Point Lookout to free the Confederates there, was ordered by Early to abandon that mission and rejoin him.

The Federals did not know of Early's decision, of course, and they expected to do battle for the city. With large contingents of VI Corps and XIX Corps in place, confidence had returned to the general population overnight; civilians in a holiday mood flocked to the fortifications to watch the contest. General Wright's wife, escorting some ladies and gentlemen of society and several members of Congress and the Cabinet, joyously cheered every Federal movement as the armies jabbed at each other.

At midafternoon the President and Mrs. Lincoln drove up to Fort Stevens in a carriage. General Wright went out to welcome his commander and, he remembered, "thoughtlessly invited him to see the fight in which we were about to engage, without for a moment supposing he would accept. A moment after, I would have given much to have recalled my words."

It was, said Lincoln eagerly, his first opportunity to see a real battle, and he took a position beside Wright on the parapet of the fort, exposed from the waist up to Confederate fire. Wright pleaded in vain that Lincoln take cover. A member of the President's cavalry escort wrote later that bullets "were sending little spurts and puffs of dust from the embankment on which he stood."

THE BATTLE OF FORT STEVEN'S
JULY 12, 1864

FROM MEMORY
W.E.RUGGLES,122/REGT.N.Y.

President and Mrs. Lincoln, like figures on a wedding cake, observe the repulse of Early's Confederates from the wall of Fort Stevens in this somewhat fanciful postwar drawing. The President did stand for a time atop the wall, but he was accompanied by General Wright and other officers; Mary Todd Lincoln remained prudently under cover.

An Ohio soldier who saw Lincoln there wrote, "In his long, yellowish linen coat and unbrushed high hat, he looked like a care worn farmer in time of peril from drouth and famine." When a busy young lieutenant colonel named Oliver Wendell Holmes Jr. saw this unprepossessing civilian standing in the spray of bullets, he snapped: "Get down, you damn fool, before you get shot." Only then did the future Supreme Court justice realize whom he was addressing. Lincoln compromised, sitting behind the parapet instead of standing on it. Still, he continually leaped up to see what was happening.

As Lincoln watched, Brigadier General Frank Wheaton launched a Federal reconnaissance in force in preparation for an all-out attack. "Our brave men charged handsomely, for they meant business and knew how it was done," wrote Major Aldace F. Walker of the VI Corps's Vermont Brigade.

The Confederates did not make it easy for them. Heavy fighting continued until well after dark. Most of the roughly 600 men killed or wounded in the two-day confrontation fell in the final fighting. It was, Walker wrote, "a bitter little contest."

Early called his commanders together later that night to give orders for the withdrawal to Virginia. "He seemed in a droll humor, perhaps one of relief," Henry Kyd Douglas remembered, "for he said to me in his falsetto drawl: 'Major, we haven't taken Washington, but we've scared Abe Lincoln like hell!' "

Lincoln had shown no fear, but the Union had been shaken to the core. The tremors affected not only politics but also the economy: On July 11 the Federal dollar reached its lowest value of the War — 39 cents. Colonel David Strother wrote in his diary, "The great financial crash which is rapidly ap-

Cross-Country Volunteers

The 2nd Massachusetts Cavalry, which hastened to resist Jubal Early's assault on Washington, included five companies of horsemen who had come from the opposite side of the continent to fight for the Union. Many of these volunteers, known as the California Hundred and the California Battalion, had been born in the East and had gone West to seek their fortunes. In 1863 they used the $200 bounty that Massachusetts offered to enlistees to pay their steamship fares from San Francisco back to Boston.

The pressures of combat soon fused the hybrid regiment into an effective unit, but the Californians kept their elaborate brass cap badge, seen on the kepi at left, and fought under their own grizzly-bear guidon (*above*).

**A PRIVATE OF THE
CALIFORNIA BATTALION**

proaching and the despairing fury of the Rebel armies may yet accomplish our ruin."

Shortly after Early issued the order, the Confederates quietly slipped away. Not knowing whether General Hunter and Brigadier General Albion P. Howe, who had just relieved Sigel, had reached the mountain passes in pursuit of him, Early did not retrace his steps but marched westward, parallel to the Potomac River. On the morning of July 14, he crossed the river at White's Ford, 30 miles from Washington, and rested his men at nearby Leesburg. In two furious

weeks he had marched to the threshold of the Union's capital and the summit of his personal glory. Now began the long retreat.

On the day Early reached Leesburg, General Hunter reappeared at Harpers Ferry. On foot and by river steamer and railroad, he and his men had been making a circuit from Lynchburg west to Charleston, West Virginia, north to Parkersburg and then back east to Harpers Ferry. Along the way, Hunter had continued his practice of burning homes, including the house of his cousin Andrew Hunter, a prominent Charles Town lawyer, and that of Edmund I. Lee, a cousin of the Confederate general. On the 20th of July, Mrs. Edmund Lee wrote Hunter a sulfurous letter. "Hyena-like you have torn my heart to pieces," she wrote, "and demonlike you have done it without a pretext of revenge, for I never harmed you." She could not even ask God to forgive him: "Were it possible for human lips to raise your name heavenward, angels would thrust the foul thing back."

On his arrival in Harpers Ferry, Hunter found orders waiting that instructed him to send his army to help VI Corps chase Early. But Grant had decided that General Wright, who was junior in grade to Hunter, should have "supreme command of all troops moving out against the enemy." Hunter immediately asked to be relieved, Colonel Strother recorded, "considering himself insulted by the proposition."

Once again, Hunter protested directly to Lincoln, and once again he was curtly rebuffed. Hunter was to remain in command of the department and turn his troops over to General Crook, who would report with them to Wright. Hunter raged, but he obeyed.

Meanwhile, General Wright with his two divisions had followed Early to Leesburg, skirmishing there on July 17 with the Confederate rear guard. Wright's force was joined by Ricketts' VI Corps division and another division from XIX Corps under Brigadier General William H. Emory. But without cavalry to force Early to stop and deploy, the infantry could do little more than march along in the raiders' footsteps.

By the 17th, however, Crook was at Purcellville, Virginia, seven miles due west of Leesburg, with Brigadier General Jeremiah Sullivan's 7,000 infantrymen and General Duffié's 2,000 troopers. For a few hours it seemed that Wright and Crook might catch Early between them. But the Confederates slipped through Snicker's Gap in the Blue Ridge Mountains — eight miles west and slightly south of Purcellville — and camped at Berryville, just west of the Shenandoah River. The next day Crook, with Wright's command in close pursuit, followed them through the gap.

While Crook's troops were crossing the Shenandoah, or the "Shining Door," as they liked to call it, Early smashed into them with his whole force. The West Virginians, in the words of one soldier, "were driven back in intense disgust." They suffered 422 casualties in a short but fierce skirmish. Wright showed no eagerness to engage the enemy that had at last deployed to face him. Instead, he spent the next day looking for another way across the river. Hunter, despite having washed his hands of the whole affair and having predicted its failure, saw a chance to help and did so at once.

William Averell's cavalry and the rest of Crook's infantry had just arrived at Harpers Ferry, and Hunter sent them south to attack Early's flanks. Colonel Rutherford B. Hayes, with the infantry, was stopped 10 miles from Snicker's Ferry on the 19th, but Averell drove toward Winchester and by late in the day had reached Stephenson's Depot, six miles from the city and well behind the Confederate position. That night, Early, threatened from three directions, marched most of his army south toward Strasburg. But he sent Ramseur's division to stop Averell. Ramseur, who had just written to his wife "I may be pardoned for saying that I am making a reputation as Major General," advanced confidently. Late in the afternoon on

the 20th, acting on an erroneous report that the enemy's numbers were small, he formed a line of battle and pitched into Averell's force north of Winchester.

Too late Ramseur realized that he was out-manned, that he was facing infantry as well as cavalry, and that the Federal line over-lapped his left by 200 yards. He tried to shift his reserve brigade to meet the threat, but before it could get into position the Confederate left "broke and ran like sheep," as the mortified Ramseur put it later. He lost 203 killed and wounded, along with four guns and more than 250 men captured by the Federals. "My men behaved shamefully," Ramseur said, and he burned for a chance to remove the blotch from his record.

By the evening of July 22, Early had reconcentrated his army at Strasburg. On that day Crook joined Averell and Hayes at Kernstown, about four miles south of Winchester. With this considerable army once again between Early and Washington, there appeared to be no further need for the VI and XIX Corps reinforcements. In fact, acting on Grant's instructions that they follow Early only long enough to be sure that the Confederates were headed back to Richmond, General Wright had rather abruptly done an about-face on July 20 and headed for Washington.

Defending the Valley was once again

Hunter's job as commander of the department. Grant explained carefully to Halleck what he wanted Hunter to do: follow Early, if possible as far south as Gordonsville and Charlottesville, where he should cut the railroads. Failing that, Hunter should at least render the Shenandoah Valley useless to the enemy. "I do not mean that houses should be burned," Grant emphasized — somewhat tardily — "but every particle of provisions and stock should be removed."

Then Grant elaborated with a metaphor that the people of the Shenandoah would never forget: Hunter's troops, he said, should "eat out Virginia clear and clean as far as they go, so that crows flying over it for the balance of the season will have to carry their provender with them."

On July 23, with Jubal Early apparently in full retreat before Crook's force at Kernstown, the canny Lincoln asked Hunter, who was still in Harpers Ferry, a prophetic question: "Are you able to take care of the enemy when he turns back on you, as he probably will, on finding that Wright has left?" The answer came the next day.

Informed on the morning of the 24th that a sizable enemy force was approaching Kernstown, General Crook assumed it to be a reconnaissance in force and moved to drive it off. He had just reorganized his 12,000 infantrymen into three divisions, commanded

Early's troops cross the Potomac River at White's Ford on July 14, returning to Virginia after failing to capture the Federal capital. During his foray into the North, Early had resupplied his army with captured horses and beef cattle and had collected cash ransoms from Hagerstown and Frederick. But the mission had cost him more than 1,000 men killed or wounded — about a tenth of his total force.

Colonel James A. Mulligan (*below*), flamboyant commander of the 23rd Illinois, known as Chicago's Irish Brigade, was mortally wounded at the Second Battle of Kernstown. Mulligan exhorted his men to save the flag, and his 19-year-old brother-in-law, Lieutenant James H. Nugent (*right*), clutched the threatened banner until he too was shot down.

by Colonels Joseph Thoburn, Isaac H. Duval and James Mulligan — the last a spirited Irish-American who wore a green scarf in combat. While Crook's infantry formed a line covering the Valley Turnpike, Averell's and Duffié's cavalry shielded his flanks.

When a Confederate assault line appeared about noon, Mulligan's division confidently charged. But instead of a reconnaissance, the Federals ran into Gordon's full division. The surprised Federals fell back to their lines. To make a flanking attack, Crook brought Thoburn's men up from reserve and waited for Averell, who had been sent around the Confederate right.

But Averell dawdled, and before he was in position the Federal infantry was caught in the jaws of a double envelopment, with Ramseur's division swinging around the right and Breckinridge's two brigades attacking on the left. Under vicious fire, the Federal line began to fold. Colonel Mulligan fell from his horse with five Minié balls in his body. As his distraught men carried their mortally wounded commander to the shade of an oak tree, Mulligan snapped, "Lay me down and save the colors."

Averell saw Breckinridge's attack, but to Crook's disgust, he simply led his men to the rear, toward Winchester. Gordon charged the center, and the Federal line gave way entirely. Crook and his officers managed to keep the retreat from becoming a full-fledged rout, but they could not stop it. The Federals fell back through Winchester to Bunker Hill, 12 miles farther north.

Once more the Shenandoah had become a valley of humiliation for the Federals. The next day, in a driving rain, Crook's men trudged through Martinsburg to the Potomac, and on the 26th they crossed into Maryland and camped at Sharpsburg to guard the South Mountain passes.

Triumphant, Early tore up the recently repaired B & O Railroad track at Martinsburg and dispatched two of his cavalry brigades, under McCausland and Bradley Johnson, raiding into Maryland and Pennsylvania. On July 30, the raiders occupied Chambersburg, Pennsylvania, and demanded $100,000 in gold as a reprisal for Hunter's latest depredations in the Shenandoah. When the town fathers failed to raise the money, McCausland burned the town.

The mission soon backfired, however. Averell's Federal cavalry pursued the raiders and surprised them with a dawn attack on August 7 near Moorefield, West Virginia. The Confederates were routed, suffering more than 500 casualties and the loss of four guns and almost 700 horses. This damaging blow to Early's cavalry, already under-strength, would have a telling effect in the fighting to come.

The Torching of Chambersburg

The sun had barely risen on July 30, 1864, when 831 Confederate cavalrymen moved unopposed into the prosperous farming and manufacturing town of Chambersburg, Pennsylvania. On a hill west of town, 2,000 additional troops waited in line of battle.

The Confederates' 28-year-old commander, Brigadier General John McCausland, demanded a ransom from the town fathers: $100,000 in gold or $500,000 in greenbacks. When he did not receive it, he ordered Chambersburg burned. "Flames burst out almost simultaneously in every part of the town," wrote a witness. Another said that for most of the inhabitants, "the first warning of danger was the kindling of the fire in their houses, and even the few articles that some caught up in their flight

were seized by the soldiers and flung back into the flames."

Chambersburg had felt the sting of war before, enduring two raids and temporary occupation; but nothing had prepared the townspeople for McCausland's ruthlessness. Another Confederate general had exhibited "some honorable traits when here," remembered one citizen, "but if McCaus-land had any he did not manifest them."

The burning of Chambersburg brought the Confederates no military gain — nor was any intended. General Jubal Early, who had conceived the raid, reported later that his sole purpose was to retaliate for the fiery destruction of civilian property wrought by Union General David Hunter that summer in the Shenandoah Valley.

Chambersburg residents examine the burned-out ruins along South Main Street, seen from the Diamond, the town's unusual 12-sided central square. In the distance rises the spire of Zion's Reformed Church, which was spared by the Confederates. A distorted pharmacy bottle (inset), retrieved from the ruins, bears witness to the intensity of the fire.

The Greek-revivalist county courthouse, shown here before the fire, was to have been the focus of Chambersburg's centennial celebration in 1864; instead, the townspeople had to rebuild it. Incorporating some of the original walls, they finished the restoration in 1865.

Rubble fills the yard beneath the surviving columns of the Franklin County Court House, one of the first buildings torched in Chambersburg. Confederates of Major Harry Gilmor's 2nd Maryland Cavalry applied barrels of kerosene, taken from a nearby grocery, to make sure the fire spread swiftly.

Only the shells of houses and shops remain at the corner of Main and King Streets. Nearly 300 buildings were destroyed, and a third of the town's 6,000 people were left homeless. The angry citizens killed three Confederates; one resident died in the fire — and three babies were born in the town that day.

The charred walls at right, below, were part of the Franklin House hotel, where General McCausland and his staff had breakfasted before burning the town. The stone pillars next door mark the site of the Bank of Chambersburg. Soon after the fire, the bank reopened for business, first in a private home and then in the Masonic Hall, which had been spared by a Confederate who was a Mason.

The remains of the W. F. Eyster &
Bro. Foundry stand at right, above,
on the Conococheague Creek. Beyond the footbridge is the Bethel
Church of God, set on fire because
the Confederates thought it was a
church for blacks. One other church
was burned because it had served as a
headquarters for Federal draftees.

"I Want Sheridan"

"He was a wonderful man on the battlefield, and never in as good humor as when under fire. This pre-supposes, however, that everyone about was doing his duty as he deemed it should be done. If he judged the contrary, one might as well be in the path of a Kansas cyclone."

CAPTAIN GEORGE SANFORD, 1ST U.S. CAVALRY, DESCRIBING MAJOR GENERAL PHILIP H. SHERIDAN

On July 31, 1864, General U. S. Grant and President Lincoln had a long, private meeting at Fort Monroe, Virginia. It was a dark moment for the Union war effort. General Jubal Early and his Confederates had been prevented from capturing Washington only at the eleventh hour, and "Old Jube" was still at large, causing havoc. Virtually all of the Shenandoah Valley was back in Confederate hands, mocking every Federal effort to seize it. For three weeks, Grant had been trying to get someone to take charge of the army units in and around Washington and chase Early to ground. But his attempts to create a unified command had been snarled in the tangle of the four separate military departments into which the area from Washington to West Virginia — including the vital Shenandoah — had been divided.

Frustrated beyond endurance, Grant had appealed directly to the President. "All I ask," Grant implored, "is that one general officer, in whom I and yourself have confidence, should command the whole." Immediately, Lincoln had set out for Fort Monroe to meet his general in chief.

Neither man ever spoke later about what they discussed. But ensuing events testify to an even closer alliance between the two rough-hewn Westerners. The next morning, Grant informed chief of staff Henry Halleck that he was sending north the commander of the Army of the Potomac's Cavalry Corps, 33-year-old Major General Philip H. Sheridan, and that the four departments should be merged into one. Major General David Hunter, as the senior officer in the region, could stay on as the administrative head of the new department. But, wrote Grant bluntly, "I want Sheridan put in command of all the troops in the field, with instructions to put himself south of the enemy and follow him to the death."

Grant knew Secretary of War Edwin M. Stanton would disapprove, thinking Sheridan too young. And he expected Stanton and Halleck to resist the idea of having a Federal army chase the Confederates deep into the Shenandoah — let alone advance south of the enemy. "It seemed to be the policy of General Halleck and Secretary Stanton," Grant wrote later, "to keep any force sent there, in pursuit of the invading army, moving right and left so as to keep between the enemy and our capital."

But now Grant had powerful support for his views. Back in Washington, Lincoln pronounced Grant's orders concerning Sheridan "exactly right," then offered his top general a bit of presidential wisdom. Do not count on the War Department, he wrote, to help prosecute a vigorous campaign in the Shenandoah. "I repeat to you it will neither be done nor attempted, unless you watch it every day and hour and force it."

Lincoln's advice fell on receptive ears. Two hours after receiving it, Grant was aboard a steamer headed north. On the eve-

This silver-and-enamel badge on a ribbon of silk, with crossed swords against a blue background, was worn over the heart by officers of the 3rd Division of Major General Philip H. Sheridan's Cavalry Corps. Officers of the 1st and 2nd Divisions wore similar badges with backgrounds of red and white. Sheridan adopted the badges to build esprit de corps.

ning of August 5, he strode into General Hunter's headquarters at Monocacy Junction, 32 miles northwest of Washington. Grant's first question: Where was the enemy? Hunter had no idea.

This was neither new nor entirely Hunter's fault. He had been trying to deal with an agile enemy for more than a month while receiving a stream of conflicting orders from Washington. And now Halleck had sent him every infantry unit within reach, including most of two corps, VI and XIX Corps. Faced with organizing an army swollen to about 30,000 men, Hunter had had little time to determine the location of Early's men.

Grant did not know where Early was either, but he knew how to find out. He ordered a concentration of all the Federal forces near Harpers Ferry. If Early was still in Maryland or Pennsylvania, then the Federals would be south of him and could cut him off. If not, they could chase him south through the Shenandoah Valley. The general in chief wanted Early stopped, and he was going to make sure it happened.

Grant wrote out lengthy instructions for Hunter. "Nothing should be left to invite the enemy to return. Take all provisions, forage and stock wanted for the use of your command. Such as cannot be consumed, destroy." But, he added, "I do not mean that houses should be destroyed."

The moment that Hunter learned he was to be merely the department administrator and was to pass the orders to Sheridan for execution, he asked to be relieved. Grant called Hunter a "brave old soldier," saying his willingness to stand aside was selfless and patriotic. But he immediately granted Hunter's request.

Now things fell rapidly into line. Sheridan arrived at Monocacy Junction on August 6 and was admonished by Grant, as one of Grant's aides recalled it, to "drive Early out of the Valley and to receive orders from no live man but Grant himself." The next day, August 7, the Administration officially merged the four military departments into the Middle Military Division and placed Sheridan in full command.

That same day, Sheridan took the reins of the Army of the Shenandoah. His force would consist of about 37,000 men when fully assembled. Sheridan's infantry included General Horatio Wright's veteran VI Corps, one division and a portion of another from General William Emory's XIX Corps, and General George Crook's division-size Army of West Virginia — which was officially redesignated VIII Corps.

Sheridan brought along with him from the Army of the Potomac two divisions of cavalry that, with William Averell's division, constituted a corps. Ignoring the fact of Averell's seniority, Sheridan named as his chief of cavalry one of the several young officers who had come with him: Brigadier General Alfred T. A. Torbert, whom Sheridan had known at West Point.

On August 10, Sheridan briskly marched his army south toward Winchester to "make the first move for the possession of the Shenandoah Valley." His next steps, however, would appear to many observers to be uncertain. Five weeks would pass while the Army of the Shenandoah advanced and retreated, probing for Confederate weaknesses. Sheridan's style appeared to be simply more of the familiar Federal timidity — so much so that several people, most notably Jubal Early, began to form seriously mistaken opinions of Little Phil Sheridan.

Sheridan had won his stars the hard way. The undersize son of Irish immigrant parents and an indifferent scholar, the 17-year-old Sheridan was working as a clerk in his hometown of Somerset, Ohio, when he wangled an appointment to the U.S. Military Academy in 1848. His dogged determination got him through, despite a hair-trigger temper that earned him so many demerits he almost failed to graduate.

One day on the parade ground, Sheridan lunged with a bayonet at a cadet sergeant who had given him a command in what Sheridan considered to be an insolent tone of voice. "My better judgement recalled me before actual contact could be made,"

General Sheridan, standing at far left, confers with four of his top subordinates, Wesley Merritt, George Crook, James W. Forsyth and George A. Custer (left to right), in this postwar photograph. All four men became famous Indian fighters, and Merritt, as a 64-year-old, led the first Philippine expedition of the Spanish-American War in 1898.

Sheridan wrote afterward. When the sergeant reported him, Sheridan attacked his adversary with his fists. For this breach of discipline, he was suspended from the academy for an entire year.

Finally graduating in 1853, Sheridan stayed in the Regular Army through eight dreary years of frontier garrison duty while many of his fellow officers were resigning their commissions to take up better-paying pursuits. When the War began, he served first as a commissary officer in Missouri and Tennessee, then as a quartermaster. In May 1862, he was promoted to colonel and was given a regiment of cavalry. Immediately, he led his men on a raid into Mississippi. His aggressiveness was such that in July five generals wired then general in chief Halleck a brief but eloquent argument for promoting Sheridan: "Brigadiers scarce; good ones scarcer. He is worth his weight in gold." Sheridan got his star.

He pinned on his second star five months later, after distinguishing himself as an infantry division commander in Tennessee during the bloody battles of Perryville and Stones River. In the fall of 1863, Sheridan fought at Chickamauga, and in November, under the admiring eye of his superior, Ulysses S. Grant, he led his division up Missionary Ridge, breaking through the enemy's defenses and leading the pursuit of the shattered Confederate Army of Tennessee. When Grant went East in the spring of 1864 to take up his duties as the new general in chief, he made only one major change in the Army of the Potomac — he insisted that Sheridan command the cavalry.

The young general soon had the chance to demonstrate his worth. In May, Sheridan led his Cavalry Corps completely around Lee's army, briefly severing the rail lines into Richmond. In the process his men not only defeated but also killed the great Confederate cavalry leader Jeb Stuart.

Sheridan had the help of a new generation of tough young cavalry officers. One was Brigadier General James H. Wilson, aged 27, who continued in charge of the division he had already commanded for a year. A second was Brigadier General Wesley Merritt, 30, who assumed command of Torbert's old division. Merritt's force included one brigade that was made up largely of Michigan troopers and led by a 24-year-old officer noted for bravado and quick thinking, Brigadier General George A. Custer.

Sheridan inspired in his men an almost mystical devotion. Captain Henry A. Du-Bois, a cavalry surgeon, marveled that although Sheridan seemed to do nothing to cultivate the esteem of his subordinates, they considered him "a brother in whom they had unlimited confidence. His appearance in front of the line of battle, without his saying a word, changed the character of every man in a moment." Captain George B. Sanford of the 1st Cavalry Division described Sheridan's influence as "like an electric shock. He was the only commander I ever met whose personal appearance in the field was an immediate and positive stimulus to battle."

Sheridan certainly did not have this effect on his officers and men because of an imposing physique. Short and thickset, he seemed to many observers to be oddly proportioned. Newspaper artist James Taylor, who looked Sheridan over carefully during the first weeks of the Valley Campaign, recorded that the new commander's "body and arms were long while his pedals were disproportionately short — 'duck legs,' in fact."

Abraham Lincoln, who took many barbs about his own appearance, was even less kind. He described Sheridan as "a brown, chunky little chap, not enough neck to hang him, and such long arms that if his ankles itch he can scratch them without stooping."

Sheridan's head was abnormally large and was misshapen by a bump in the back at the hatline. His voice croaked when he spoke and rasped when he became excited. But his fierce black eyes were penetrating, and he radiated energy and determination. Taylor summed up the ungainly Irishman as a "little mountain of combative force."

On August 6, as the Federals began to concentrate around Harpers Ferry, most of Early's soldiers were north of the Potomac, near Sharpsburg and Hagerstown, loading their wagons with just-harvested local wheat. Early quickly pulled his men and supply wagons back across the Potomac to Martinsburg and then 12 more miles to Bunker Hill. From there he could range forward to cut the B & O Railroad and startle the North whenever he wished, or he could fall back before any strong Federal advance.

When Sheridan began just such an advance on August 10, Early deftly retreated from Bunker Hill to Fisher's Hill, south of Strasburg, anchoring his right on Massanutten Mountain and his left on North Mountain, a spur of the Alleghenies four miles away. The Federals deployed along Cedar Creek, just north of Strasburg.

Now Early and Sheridan both awaited reinforcement. Wilson's cavalry and a division of XIX Corps had yet to reach Sheridan. Early was expecting Lieutenant General Richard H. Anderson with a division of infantry, led by Major General Joseph Kershaw, from the Army of Northern Virginia's battle-hardened I Corps. Also on the way from Robert E. Lee's army were a division of cavalry under Major General Fitzhugh Lee and a battalion of artillery.

Grant, thinking the entire I Corps was to reinforce Early, ordered Sheridan not to attack for the moment. Sheridan responded that the Cedar Creek position was a poor one to defend: "I cannot cover the numerous rivers that lead in on both of my flanks to the rear." Then on August 13, Colonel John S. Mosby's fast-riding Rangers destroyed a large Federal wagon train near Berryville. With only two days' rations on hand, and with a Confederate force perhaps as large as a corps approaching his army's left flank, Sheridan decided on August 16 to fall back northward to better ground.

On that day, General Wesley Merritt's Federal cavalry division was patrolling the mouth of the Luray Valley. Seeing no sign of the enemy, the troopers prepared to camp for the night a half mile north of the Shenandoah, near Front Royal. Suddenly Fitzhugh Lee's cavalry, supported by a brigade of infantry from Kershaw's division, attacked the pickets of one of Merritt's Union brigades led by Colonel Thomas Devin.

Hearing the eruption of firing, Merritt moved fast. Leaving Devin to hold Lee, he ordered Custer's brigade to hasten toward the Shenandoah where the main body of Kershaw's Confederates had been observed. Moving diagonally to their left, Custer's men soon saw that the lead Confederate units were in the act of crossing the river. Custer's troopers, soon joined by other units from Merritt's division, swiftly charged Kershaw's infantrymen, who were caught fording the Shenandoah, and sent them hurrying

Preceded by skirmishers (*middle distance*) and covered by the artillery piece on the near hillside, South Carolinians of General Joseph Kershaw's division march into the Shenandoah Valley in August 1864. The smoke on the horizon is from property set afire by the Federals.

back in confusion to the other side, leaving behind 300 prisoners. Having thus neatly slowed the advance of Jubal Early's reinforcements, Merritt's cavalry rejoined Sheridan's army, acting as rear guard during its withdrawal. Burning all the wheat, hay and provisions to be found in their path, the Federals drew off to the east side of the Valley, establishing a north-south line from near Charles Town to Berryville.

The withdrawal, reminiscent of previous retreats by skittish Federal generals, drew a torrent of public criticism down on Sheridan. The North suffered fresh agonies of fear that Early was about to start marauding in Maryland again. But as Sheridan explained to Grant, the movement was a deliberate invitation to lure the Confederates northward once more, whereupon he would be south of them and in position to spring a giant trap. Amid the cries of panic and calls for his relief, Sheridan calmly asserted to

Grant, "There is no occasion for alarm."

But Early refused Sheridan's bait. Instead, on August 21, he attacked, throwing his own corps against Sheridan's right, below Charles Town, while Anderson ordered Kershaw's infantry to assault Sheridan's left at Berryville. Anderson's movement was stopped cold by the Federal cavalry of Merritt and Wilson. At first the Confederates pushed back VI Corps in heavy fighting, but the Federal line was soon restored.

Though he had suffered serious losses in the attack and could find no weakness in Sheridan's compact defensive lines, Early still underestimated his new opponent. On August 25, assuming Sheridan would withdraw as his predecessors had done when threatened with a flanking movement, Early headed north to cross the Potomac yet again.

Kershaw's infantry and General John McCausland's cavalry opened heavy fire to hold the Federals in place while the rest of

105

Early's infantry under General John Breckinridge marched north to Shepherdstown. Sheridan suspected that the firing on his front was a diversion, however, and sent General Torbert with two divisions of cavalry to see what Early was up to.

Near Leetown, about eight miles south of Shepherdstown, Torbert's horsemen ran into the Confederate cavalrymen who were screening Breckinridge's march. Torbert attacked. His troopers brushed aside the enemy riders—only to confront Breckinridge's infantry divisions. Both sides were startled by the engagement; the Federals managed to drive back the lead Confederate units, but at heavy cost. Soon Torbert's outnumbered and outgunned troopers were fleeing toward the Potomac.

While Torbert and most of his brigades quickly got out of harm's way, George Custer's Michigan troopers got trapped between the Potomac and Breckinridge's infantry. Custer backed coolly toward the river, forestalling with sheer bravado a Confederate charge. Then, using a little-known ford, Custer's men waded across the Potomac and out of the trap. The maneuver drew cheers even from Breckinridge's men.

Early now had a clear path into Maryland, but he dared not take it. Sheridan's cavalry had discovered exactly where his army was, and the Federal infantry, camped to the east between Charles Town and Harpers Ferry, was in position to trap him. He gave up his invasion plans and returned to Bunker Hill.

On the night of August 26, Grant told Sheridan that heavy assaults by the Army of the Potomac on Confederate lines near Petersburg had inflicted 10,000 casualties on Robert E. Lee's main army in the past two weeks. Lee would have to call back the rein-

Confederate Rangers under Colonel John S. Mosby (*on white horse next to the howitzer at left*) swoop down on a Federal supply train outside Berryville on August 13, 1864, sending its infantry escort scurrying for cover. In the raid, which began with three shots from the howitzer, 208 prisoners were taken and nearly 100 wagons and their contents were destroyed.

forcements he had sent Early, Grant predicted. "Watch closely, and if you find this thing correct, push with all vigor."

Sheridan had his army re-form the north-south line from Charles Town to Berryville and waited. When Halleck relayed a rumor that Breckinridge had been detached to raid in West Virginia, Sheridan's response was steely: "I believe no troops have yet left the Valley, but I believe they will, and that it will be their last campaign in the Shenandoah."

Sheridan had hardly sent the dispatch when, as predicted, Lee recalled Anderson and Kershaw to eastern Virginia. On September 3, Kershaw's division of I Corps marched east from Winchester toward Berryville, heading for passes through the Blue Ridge Mountains. At the same moment,

George Crook was moving his VIII Corps, as Sheridan had ordered, into its former position in front of Berryville on the left of the Federal line. A fight was inevitable.

It came at sunset, just as the Federals were going into camp. Kershaw's infantry, stumbling into Crook's skirmishers, recoiled at first but recovered from their surprise and attacked. Crook's men also fell back in confusion only to rally and repulse the Confederates. Before darkness ended the fierce little clash, the Federals had driven Kershaw and his men back toward Winchester.

At dawn the next morning, Early arrived with reinforcements, intending to attack. But when he saw Sheridan's whole army entrenched from Berryville northward, he pulled his entire force back to Winchester

The Fighting Butterflies

Among the rough-and-ready horsemen of Sheridan's Cavalry Corps, the 3rd New Jersey was decidedly out of the ordinary, at least in its resplendent appearance. To attract recruits, New Jersey authorities had outfitted the unit in a distinctive uniform — visorless forage cap, elaborately braided jacket and a hooded cloak, or *talma* — that resembled the brilliant garb worn by hussar regiments in European armies.

When the 3rd New Jersey reached the front in 1864, the gaudily clad recruits were derisively dubbed "butterflies" by the army's veterans. But the regiment proved itself as tough as any, fighting bravely under Sheridan in the Shenandoah at the battles of Winchester and Tom's Brook.

TROOPER OF THE 3RD NEW JERSEY

HUSSAR-STYLE JACKET AND *TALMA*

and formed a line facing the Federals from the high ground just east of the main north-south highway, the Valley Turnpike. Early decided to keep Kershaw with him for a few more days and see what developed.

In the vicinity of Winchester, where the armies now faced each other, the Shenandoah Valley is at its widest; the distance from North Mountain in the west to the Blue Ridge averages 20 miles. Here the Shenandoah River, its two forks united at Front Royal, flows toward the Potomac along the Valley's eastern boundary, at the foot of the Blue Ridge. Opequon Creek flows down the middle of the Valley from the Winchester area to its own confluence with the Potomac. The enemy lines were about six miles apart, equidistant from the Opequon.

While Sheridan waited for Kershaw's men to leave the Valley, he kept his cavalry active, probing and harassing the Confederate pickets. As his men were pleased to notice, Sheridan not only managed their camps and marches efficiently but also kept track — as his predecessors had sometimes neglected to do — of exactly where the enemy was located. Major Aldace F. Walker of the 11th Vermont was among his admirers: "The careful restless handling of those horsemen by our General, whose skill we were now beginning to appreciate, has never been surpassed if ever equalled."

Sheridan's aggressive patrolling was not enough, however, for U. S. Grant. Restive at all the delays, he left for Charles Town on September 14 to meet with Sheridan in person. In his pocket was a plan of campaign that would drive Early back on Richmond.

But when Grant reached Charles Town on the morning of September 16, the situation had changed. Sheridan, learning from a spy that Kershaw had left the Valley at last, was bursting with plans of his own. As the two generals paced near Sheridan's headquarters, it was the younger man who did most of the talking. Grant, impressed by what he heard, merely stuffed his notes in his pocket and confined his instructions to a two-word grunt of approval: "Go in."

Despite the loss of Kershaw's division and the presence of a superior Federal force only six miles away, General Early remained certain he retained the upper hand. He was satisfied, he wrote later, that Sheridan "was without enterprise, and possessed an excessive caution which amounted to timidity."

Confident that he would not be attacked, Early boldly divided his army to strike again at the B & O Railroad and threaten Maryland. Leaving General Stephen Ramseur's 2,400 men in front of Winchester and Brigadier General Gabriel Wharton's 1,600 at Stephenson's Depot four miles north, Early started on September 17 toward the B & O's Martinsburg yards with the divisions of Generals Robert Rodes and John Gordon. Early's headquarters staff did not share their commander's low opinion of Sheridan. They were worried, sensing that their crusty commander was courting disaster. "The air," recalled Major Henry Kyd Douglas later, "seemed to have a sulphurous smell."

Sheridan immediately decided to strike the two divisions Early had left behind near Winchester. While Wright's VI Corps and Emory's XIX Corps attacked Ramseur from the east along the road from Berryville to Winchester, two cavalry divisions under William Averell and Wesley Merritt would swing far north around Wharton's left, and Crook would march south around Ramseur's

Horsepower for the Union

By 1864, the much-maligned Union cavalry had become more than a match for its celebrated Confederate counterpart. The turnabout resulted in large part from the establishment by the U.S. government of an improved system of supplying new horses and rehabilitating worn-out ones. While horses were becoming so scarce in the South that some Confederate cavalry units had to be dismounted, six huge remount depots provided Federal troopers with a steady supply of healthy, well-trained animals. The largest depot was at Giesboro Point *(below)*, a 625-acre complex across the Potomac River from Washington, D.C., where 30,000 horses could be cared for at a time. All of them were needed. During the first eight months of 1864, the cavalry of the Army of the Potomac received two complete remounts, or nearly 40,000 horses; during the Valley Campaign, Sheridan's army alone required 150 new horses per day.

Prospective Federal cavalry horses share one of the spacious corrals at the Giesboro depot. Each corral was equipped with hayracks and watertroughs

Blacksmiths and farriers at the Giesboro depot gather in front of their shop with the tools of their trade. In 1864, these men shod 170,622 cavalry horses and more than 12,000 artillery horses.

and could accommodate more than 1,000 horses. Cavalrymen waiting to be remounted helped train and care for the animals.

right; Sheridan was going to attempt a classic double envelopment. If it succeeded, half of Early's force would be destroyed and the other half trapped in the lower Valley.

The prospective battlefield had drawbacks, however, for the attackers. Hemmed in on the north and south by two small watercourses, Redbud Run and Abraham's Creek, it was cramped and did not allow sufficient room for maneuver. Dead ahead was the larger Opequon Creek, behind which Ramseur waited on some heights just east of Winchester itself. As it meandered southeastward, Redbud Run was bordered by marshy ground and stands of timber. The Berryville road neatly bisected the field but offered only a narrow avenue down which most of the advancing Federals would have to move.

Ramseur had taken advantage of the terrain. His line, supported by a single battery, faced an open plateau. His right extended almost to the steep banks of Abraham's Creek and was screened by Major General Lunsford Lomax's cavalry. The longer expanse between his left and the marshy bed of Redbud Run was being watched by Fitzhugh Lee's division of horsemen.

On September 18, while Sheridan was preparing to attack toward Winchester at dawn the next day, Jubal Early was in Martinsburg, 20 miles to the north. There he read copies of some Federal messages found in the local telegraph office — and soon came across one that must have caused the blood to drain from his face. It referred to Grant's recent visit to Sheridan's headquarters. Grant's presence meant just one thing: action. Thoroughly alarmed, Early ordered the two divisions with him to make a forced march back to Winchester. By nightfall, Rodes had joined Wharton's division at Ste-

phenson's Depot. Gordon was still eight miles farther north, at Bunker Hill, under orders to join Rodes by daybreak.

Sheridan's Federals went into action at 3 a.m. on the 19th, opening what would become known as Third Winchester by the defenders and the Battle of Opequon Creek by the Federals. At first, all went well for Sheridan's attackers. Wilson's division of cavalry crossed the Opequon on the Berryville road, drove off a few pickets and galloped through a narrow, two-mile-long defile known as Berryville Canyon. At the western end of the canyon, the road ascended a small hill defended by skirmishers from Ramseur's division. Wilson's men easily overran this first line of Confederates, then dismounted and held the hill, thus covering the Federal infantry's route to the battlefield.

Before long, the vanguard of VI Corps arrived. Wilson's cavalry remounted and moved off to the left while VI Corps formed a line of battle under fire from Ramseur's battery a mile away. Brigadier General James Ricketts' division formed to the right of the road and Brigadier General George Washington Getty's to the left. The division led by Brigadier General David A. Russell remained in reserve.

The soldiers were impressed to see Sheridan "at the very front, and under the fire of the enemy," Major Walker of the 11th Vermont wrote later. Sitting his horse on a "conspicuous elevation," Little Phil Sheridan was "carefully attending to details which we had been accustomed to see more celebrated commanders entrust to their staff."

But Sheridan was focusing too much attention on the initial attack and not enough on the troops advancing from the rear. As a result, the rest of the Federal infantry got

The Slave and the Schoolmistress

Although she was a Quaker passivist, Rebecca I. Wright (*above*) was also a staunch Unionist. She and slave Thomas Laws, standing at her door at left, risked their lives to pass crucial information to General Sheridan.

Sheridan's decision to fight at Winchester was based on information he got through a cloak-and-dagger operation carried out by two unlikely participants — a young school mistress named Rebecca Wright and an elderly slave, Thomas Laws.

Seeking clues to enemy troop strength, Federal scouts had come across Laws at his home near Berryville. When Laws said that he had a permit to travel to and from Winchester, the scouts enlisted his help. Next, a reliable contact in Winchester had to be found. Wright was suggested by General Crook, who knew her from a previous Federal occupation of the town.

Sheridan wrote on a tissue, wad-
ded it in tin foil and told Laws to carry it in his mouth. If he was accosted by Confederates, he was to swallow the foil. Laws found Wright's home and won her trust. As luck would have it, a Confederate officer had recently confided to her that General Kershaw's division had left Early's army for Richmond. Laws carried this vital news back through the lines in the same tin foil.

"Many times during the next day, and the quiet Sabbath that followed, I wondered what had become of the messenger, and what would result from my note," Wright recalled. Her answer came early September 19, when she was awakened by the booming of Union cannon.

into a serious snarl. Contrary to Sheridan's instructions, VI Corps had brought along its full complement of supply wagons and ambulances. These blocked the narrow Berryville Canyon, bringing the advance of XIX Corps to a virtual halt. General Wright tried to get his wagons to the side of the road to make way for Emory's troops, but the result was a jam that delayed the entire assault.

Early took advantage of the Federal confusion to reorganize his position in front of Winchester. Around 10 a.m. Gordon, marching in from the north, formed a line of battle in front of a thicket just south of Redbud Run. Rodes, following close behind, filed past Gordon's men to plug the gap between them and Ramseur's division. Remaining to the north at Stephenson's Depot were Gabriel Wharton's infantry division and McCausland's cavalry, both commanded by Breckinridge. Although forced to give ground slowly under pressure from Averell's and Merritt's Federal cavalry, Breckinridge's force seemed strong enough to make an effective fighting retreat, protecting the left of Early's line.

It was noon before the Federal XIX Corps made its way out of Berryville Canyon — and by then Early's main units were in place and waiting. Nevertheless Sheridan, ordering the discharge of a signal gun, launched the main Federal attack. The men of VI Corps on the Union left, after struggling through a dense thicket, moved forward and got their first look at their objective. "The prospect was appalling," wrote Major Walker. The troops would have to advance across a long, open slope to the foot of a steep hill, then move up the hill in the face of Confederate guns located on the crest. Seeing this fearsome sight, Walker recalled, "the line invol-

untarily halted, and the men threw themselves on the ground." Then, said the chaplain of the 10th Vermont in his own account, "an iron surf, rolling in from the enemy's batteries, broke over us."

On the Federal right, XIX Corps was having greater success. Brigadier General Cuvier Grover's division, leading the charge, slammed into Gordon's left, held by Colonel Edmund Atkinson's Georgia brigade, and drove the Georgians back into some woods. There General Grover tried to halt and reorganize, but his excited troops, ignoring orders, plunged into the trees after the Confederates. They paid a heavy price for their impetuosity. Emerging from the woods, the Federals were hit by deadly close-range fire from the 12 guns of Lieutenant Colonel Carter Braxton's artillery battalion. Then, from

the right, Fitzhugh Lee's horse artillery raked the length of the Federal line, plowing lanes through the regiments.

Meanwhile, as the officers of VI Corps got their men moving again, a minor oversight in Sheridan's orders brought the Federal left to the brink of disaster. Sixth Corps had been instructed to advance along the Berryville road, which veered off sharply to the south. The men obediently followed the road, even though it meant marching left into a hail of canister from the Confederate batteries. Grimly the Federals fought their way sideways and forward, gradually bending back Ramseur's southern flank. But XIX Corps, drawn forward by their success on the right, continued straight ahead. A gap opened in the center of the Federal line — and the Confederates charged right into it.

Led by a line of skirmishers, Major General James B. Ricketts' 3rd Division charges up a wooded hill near the Berryville road about noon on September 19, 1864. The Union attack faltered when XIX Corps, on Ricketts' right, failed to advance.

The counterattack was staged by Early's hard-fighting subordinates, Gordon and Rodes. Knowing that their main infantry line would be outnumbered when Sheridan's entire force got into action, the two generals agreed that the best course of action was to charge, hoping to confuse the Federals long enough to permit their men to escape.

The attack was delayed briefly when, just as the two men finished conferring, Rodes was mortally wounded, struck behind the ear by a shell fragment. But Gordon quickly took command of both divisions and launched the desperate assault. The Confederates surged forward, screaming the Rebel yell, straight for the just-opened hole in the Federal line. The unexpected charge struck the Federal center, according to the Vermont major, Aldace Walker, "with a heavy force, crumbling off the troops on either side of it, and causing the troops on each side of the interval to think that the others had let the enemy through." Ricketts' right and Grover's entire division were driven back. Captain Henry A. DuPont, General Crook's artillery chief, was on the knoll with Sheridan when fleeing men "began to emerge from the woods, their dark blouses looking like black spots on the sunburnt vegetation." Sheridan sent his staff and escort officers galloping in all directions to try to stop the rout and to summon Crook's corps, which until now had been waiting in reserve by the Opequon. Then Sheridan simply sat his horse, DuPont recalled, watching "silent and immovable" as his infantry seemed to disintegrate.

But the situation was not as desperate as it appeared — if only because Sheridan had more than 30,000 men to Early's 14,000. General David Russell's division rushed forward from its reserve position, and though Russell had been shot in the chest, he urged his men on until another shell fragment struck him within inches of the first, tearing through his heart and killing him instantly. The three batteries of Colonel Charles H. Tompkins' artillery brigade rained shells into the advancing Confederates on VI Corps's right, bolstering that flank. Brigadier General Emory Upton, commanding Russell's 2nd Brigade, marched his men toward the gap; then, finding he was too late to plug it, placed half his command in line facing northwest, at an angle to the Confederate line of advance. These Federals — the 2nd Connecticut Heavy Artillery, serving as infantry under Colonel Ranald S. Mackenzie — fixed bayonets and waited.

Mackenzie, a tough 24-year-old West Pointer, had taken command of the 2nd Connecticut just months earlier, but the men had already learned to hate him. First Lieutenant Theodore F. Vaill remembered Mackenzie as a cruel martinet. The previous commander, Vaill wrote, "had chastised us with whips, but Mackenzie dealt in scorpions." There were rumors that some members of the regiment intended to shoot the "Perpetual Punisher," as they called Mackenzie, at the first opportunity.

But when the Confederates were within 200 yards and Upton ordered the charge, Mackenzie was transformed. Vaill described him as grinning broadly and waving his hat joyfully as he galloped through "a perfect hailstorm of rebel lead and iron, with as much impunity as though he had been a ghost. The men hated him with the hate of hell, but they could not draw a bead on so brave a man as that." With the 2nd Connecticut in the lead, Upton's brigade pinched off

Confederate Brigadier General Robert E. Rodes (*inset*) was mortally wounded at Winchester. Below, as his division retreats before the Federals along the Berryville road, the fallen commander is put in an ambulance by three of his men. Rodes's officers tried to keep his death a secret from the rank and file, fearing the news would unnerve them.

the Confederate advance, took hundreds of prisoners and restored the Federal line.

A lull now settled over the field, and General Early concluded that the fighting was over. Even years later he referred to the situation at midafternoon as "a splendid victory." But while Early smugly waited for the Federals to retire, Sheridan was energetically preparing to bag Early's entire army.

Sheridan's plan was to send Crook's infantry — now on the field after being held up in the Berryville Canyon — to the left. They would cross the Valley Turnpike south of Winchester to cut off a Confederate retreat in that direction. But Torbert had not sent word about Merritt's and Averell's cavalry

attack on the Confederate left near Stephenson's Depot. Sheridan reluctantly told Crook to go instead to the right of XIX Corps "and look well for the right flank" while Wilson's troopers moved left to feel for the southern end of the Confederate line.

About that time, as Sheridan learned shortly afterward, Averell and Merritt were approaching Early's left, driving Breckinridge's force southward along the Valley Turnpike. Around 2 p.m., one of Breckinridge's infantry brigades, led by Colonel George S. Patton, had tried to make a stand on that flank along with Fitzhugh Lee's cavalry. But they could not hold because both Confederate commanders were wounded — Patton mortally, Lee seriously.

Brigadier General David A. Russell (*right*), commander of VI Corps's 1st Division, and his subordinate, Brigadier General Emory Upton (*far right, in a postwar photograph*) were both struck down by Confederate artillery fire in the afternoon fighting. Russell was killed outright; Upton had a quarter pound of flesh ripped from his thigh, but he survived.

Breckinridge re-formed Wharton's weary division perpendicular to the pike to protect the Confederate left. But soon Early learned that Wilson's horsemen were rounding his other flank and approaching the Valley Turnpike to the south. Early detached a brigade from Lee's hard-pressed division to deal with Wilson and keep the pike open.

Early's "splendid victory" was eroding fast, and Sheridan's double envelopment was nearly accomplished as Crook prepared the final thrust. Having placed Colonel Joseph Thoburn's division between XIX Corps's right and Redbud Run, Crook led his other division, under Colonel Isaac H. Duval, north across the stream — and discovered he was beyond the Confederate left flank. Instantly, Crook ordered an attack.

Sheridan got word of Crook's preparations when he learned that Wilson's cavalrymen were pressuring the Confederate right. The time had come for a last, crushing attack. Galloping over to Thoburn's position, Sheridan ordered his division to advance and sent messages instructing XIX Corps and part of VI Corps to wheel forward also, maintaining alignment with Duval's division.

This done, Sheridan returned to his command post, riding along the lines of VI Corps and XIX Corps. Normally, a commanding general would make that ride well to the rear. But the astonished Major Walker saw Sheridan gallop "along the whole of our extended *skirmish line*, wheeling out from the storm of bullets only as he reached our own division, and pausing as he passed between the brigades to exclaim, with eloquent profanity, 'Crook and Averell are on their left and rear — we've got 'em bagged, by God!'"

Crook's "broad blue waves surged forward with a yell that lasted for minutes," wrote Captain John DeForest of XIX Corps.

117

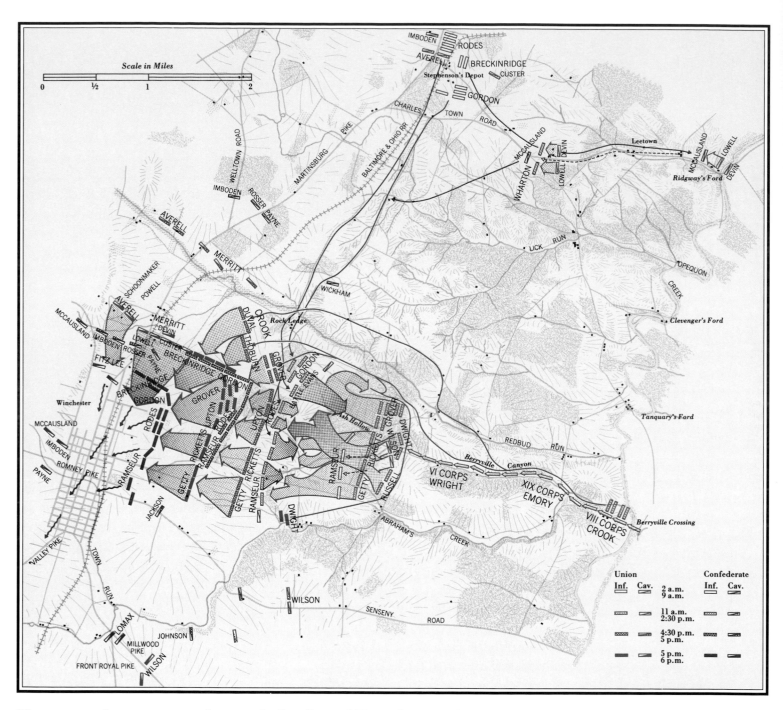

Scale in Miles
0   ½   1   2

Union   Confederate
Inf. Cav.   2 a.m.   Inf. Cav.
                9 a.m.

                11 a.m.
                2:30 p.m.

                4:30 p.m.
                5 p.m.

                5 p.m.
                6 p.m.

"In response there arose a continuous, deafening wail of musketry. For a time I despaired of the success of the attack, for it did not seem possible that any troops could endure such fire. But the yell came steadily on and triumphed over the fusillade."

When Duval's men had struggled through the swamps along Redbud Run and had linked with Thoburn's line, General Crook rode over to see why XIX Corps was not keeping pace with the advance. He found

General Emory's men still pinned down by Braxton's 12-gun artillery battalion, posted at the center of the Confederate line.

"The shells have an awful, unearthly, hissing sound," recalled Private Herbert Hill of the 8th Vermont. "A tall man near me receives a bad gash in his forehead; the crimson blood flows down his face and bosom. Another has his chin shot away, leaving his tongue dangling exposed over his throat."

Crook could not find General Emory; in-

After nearly eight hours of see-saw fighting on September 19, the Confederate divisions of Breckinridge, Rodes, Gordon and Ramseur had been forced into an L-shaped defensive perimeter northeast of Winchester. About 4:30 p.m., Crook's VIII Corps and Wright's VI Corps, supported by the cavalry divisions of Merritt and Averell, attacked the perimeter. Merritt's charge broke through Breckinridge's line, precipitating a Confederate rout.

Men of General George Crook's VIII Corps storm an earthwork on the Confederate left flank during the climactic fighting late in the afternoon. "The whole command, cheering as they went, rushed on heedless of the destructive fire," Crook reported, "all seemingly intent on one grand object, the total and complete rout of the enemy."

stead he found General Upton, from VI Corps, desperately trying to get XIX Corps moving. At length Upton gave up and deployed his own right in front of XIX Corps, joining Crook's line, and advanced. A shell fragment tore through his thigh, knocking him from his horse and laying bare his femoral artery. Ignoring the terrible wound, Upton refused to leave the field. Once a surgeon had stopped the bleeding, he ordered himself put on a stretcher and carried along with his men. Upton's action, said a fellow officer, was "the most heroic that came under my observation during the war."

Slowly the tide of battle began to turn in the Federals' favor. Ramseur's and Rodes's divisions, hearing the roar of Breckinridge's battle with Crook in their rear, began falling back toward Winchester. Sensing the kill, Sheridan galloped along the Federal lines, waving his hat and exhorting his infantry forward. Now it was the Confederates who suffered heavy losses. On Gordon's left flank, the remnants of the Stonewall Brigade with-

drew, leaving their commander, Colonel John H. Funk, dying within a mile of his family home. In the center, Braxton's guns limbered up to retreat in a deadly cross fire that killed gunners and brought horses thrashing to the ground. Nearby, Brigadier General Archibald Godwin, who was commanding one of Ramseur's brigades, fell with a fatal wound in the neck.

Then came the coup de grâce — a thundering cavalry charge by Merritt and Averell. Captain S. E. Howard of the 8th Vermont looked to his right and saw "a sight to be remembered a lifetime. In solid columns, with drawn sabers flashing in the sun, and without firing a shot, down from the crest in the left rear of the enemy came a brigade of troopers, and burst at a gallop upon the surprised enemy. It was like a thunder-clap out of a clear sky, and the bolt struck home."

While Averell's division galloped around the Confederate left to strike at the enemy rear, Merritt hurled his horsemen on the line of earthworks held by Breckinridge just north of Winchester. Colonel Thomas Devin's brigade, said Merritt, "burst like a storm of case-shot in their midst, showering saber blows on their heads and shoulders, trampling them under, and routing them in droves in every direction." Next, Merritt sent the brigade commanded by a young Boston blue blood, Colonel Charles Russell Lowell, charging for a two-gun redoubt in the center of Breckinridge's line. Just as the horsemen reached it, the cannon roared, smashing a dozen horsemen to the ground. A staff officer riding next to Lowell had his arm torn off, and Lowell lost his fourth horse of the day. But the charge could not be stopped, and the redoubt was taken. "It was a noble work well done," Merritt reported, "a theme for the poet; a scene for the painter." The Confederate line disintegrated, with Merritt's troopers pursuing fugitives into the streets of Winchester. "During the war the saber has never reaped such a harvest as on that day," onc cavalryman recalled.

Confederate Captain Robert E. Park of the 12th Alabama was lying wounded in a Winchester hotel. He wrote in his diary that Federal shells were crashing into the building and "knocking down bricks, plastering, planks and splinters over the helpless wounded and dying." Before long, he wrote, "our scattered troops, closely followed by the large army of pursuers, retreated rapidly and in disorder through the city. It was a sad, humiliating sight." With night falling, the battered town of Winchester changed hands for the 73rd and final time in the War.

As General Gordon rode into the maelstrom of fleeing men, wagons and guns in the streets of Winchester shouting "Georgians never run from a battlefield!" he received another shock. "To my horror," he wrote

Colonel James M. Schoonmaker (*on white horse*) leads the 1st Brigade of Averell's cavalry division in the victorious charge against Confederate earthworks outside Winchester. "It was a magnificent scene," a Pennsylvania trooper said, "one moving mass of glittering sabers, interspersed with brilliant brigade and regimental colors and battle flags."

later, he found his wife — as well as Mrs. Breckinridge and the wives of other officers — "on the street, where shells from Sheridan's batteries were falling and Minie balls flying." She was pleading with her husband's troops to keep fighting. General Gordon had to leave her there with their six-year-old son, presuming they would be captured. But Mrs. Gordon talked some soldiers into hitching up her carriage, and she and her son escaped, along with Mrs. Breckinridge.

The Federal cavalry and Crook's infantry chased the Confederates south for a few miles. General Ramseur, whose exhausted men had met the Federals' first attack, covered the retreat. Their courage in the midst of disaster restored the reputation that had been tarnished the previous month at Stephenson's Depot.

Darkness put an end to the chase. As night fell, Sheridan rode into the town and reported the victory to Washington in a matter-of-fact telegram. Then he sent another message to his chief of staff, Lieutenant Colonel James Forsyth, that in ringing phrases signaled an end to Federal humiliation in the Shenandoah: "We have just sent them awhirling through Winchester, and we are after them tomorrow."

Another wire reached General Grant, provoking the only show of exhilaration his staff officers had ever seen. "He came out of his tent," one officer recalled, "threw his hat in the air, and went back in again. He knew that was the beginning of the end."

It was an awful night for the Confederates, General Gordon later wrote: "Drearily and silently, with burdened brains and aching hearts, leaving our dead and many of our wounded behind us, we rode hour after

hour." Early had lost more than one quarter of his entire army — about 4,000 men, half of them prisoners. Although the Confederates had inflicted heavy punishment on Sheridan's attackers — 5,018 casualties, 80 percent of them killed or wounded — the Federal losses were proportionately smaller and much more easily replaced.

But Jubal Early never admitted defeat. Years later he charged, "Sheridan ought to have been cashiered" for letting the Confederates escape with three fourths of their men. The next day he posted his survivors in the formidable line at Fisher's Hill, known as the Gibraltar of the Valley, where he had faced down Sheridan once before.

From abrupt cliffs looming over the Valley pike, a steep, densely wooded ridge extended east to the nose of Massanutten Mountain. Cleared and somewhat gentler ridges stretched west to North Mountain. Fully manned, Fisher's Hill was virtually impregnable. But Early was increasingly short of men and officers.

He had put Ramseur in charge of Rodes's division, giving Ramseur's division to Brigadier General John Pegram. But at Fisher's Hill, Early received another blow; Lee had ordered Breckinridge south, to resume command of the Department of Western Virginia. Thus Early had to prepare his defenses without two of his best subordinates.

As Sheridan advanced through Strasburg, Early massed infantry and artillery on either side of the depression in Fisher's Hill through which the Valley pike wound south. He left the western end of the line more lightly defended by Lunsford Lomax's dismounted cavalry. Fitzhugh Lee's cavalry he sent into the Luray Valley to keep the Federals from flanking his right by advancing

The three officers at right were among the 4,000 casualties suffered by the Confederates at Winchester. Wills was killed instantly by the concussion of an exploding artillery shell; Patton and Blacknall were mortally wounded, and both died as prisoners of war.

A dog mourns the body of his master, a soldier in General Ramseur's division, in a grove north of the Berryville road. Artist James E. Taylor, who drew the scene for a Northern newspaper the day after the battle, noted that the dog resisted "the friendly overtures of the touched Federals, allowing none to approach while keeping a steadfast watch over his dead."

COLONEL GEORGE S. PATTON
Echols' Brigade

LIEUTENANT GEORGE W. WILLS
43rd North Carolina

COLONEL CHARLES C. BLACKNALL
23rd North Carolina

on the other side of Massanutten Mountain.

Sheridan was in no hurry. Fisher's Hill was too rugged for a frontal assault. Crook proposed another turning movement against Early's left. At a council of war that evening, Crook introduced a smoother speaker— Colonel Rutherford B. Hayes—to advance his arguments. Apparently Hayes was persuasive; Sheridan agreed to the plan.

The Federals were in full view of a Confederate signal station atop Shenandoah Peak, the northernmost eminence of Massanutten Mountain. In order to elude surveillance, Crook kept his corps hidden all day on September 21 and began his march to North Mountain under cover of darkness. Moving slowly, he took most of the next day to get into position. Meanwhile, Sheridan sent Torbert with two cavalry divisions east around the Massanutten to cross the mountain at New Market Gap and cut off Early's line of retreat.

On September 22, Sheridan deployed his VI and XIX Corps formations noisily and visibly before Fisher's Hill, where Early awaited attack with decreasing confidence. By late afternoon, Early concluded that his force "was not strong enough to resist a determined assault." He ordered a withdrawal after dark. But at dusk, Crook's ranks appeared from the woods of North Mountain, marching east, rolling up Lomax's thin line. The same maneuver had driven the Confederates from Winchester, yet it took them completely by surprise. "Had the heavens opened and we been seen descending from the clouds," a Federal officer wrote, "no greater consternation would have been created." In moments, Crook's left connected with VI Corps's right and the Federals swarmed over the breastworks.

"The mischief could not be repaired," Early admitted grudgingly. For the second time in three days his army was routed. He had lost another 1,200 men, most of them taken prisoner, and had been forced to abandon 20 guns. His remaining force was now in imminent danger of total destruction.

All night long the Federals hounded Early's shattered brigades southward. "Run, boys, run!" Sheridan bellowed to his men as he led them up the Valley pike. "Don't wait to form! Don't let 'em stop." When some soldiers protested that they were too exhausted to continue, he shot back, "If you can't run, then holler!"

Five miles from Fisher's Hill, the Confederates posted two guns on high ground and tried to make a stand, but they were soon overwhelmed. Among those killed that night was one of the Confederacy's best-loved officers—chief of staff to Stonewall Jackson, Richard Ewell and Jubal Early—Lieutenant Colonel Alexander S. (Sandie) Pendleton.

When he entered Woodstock, nine miles from Fisher's Hill, at dawn, Sheridan figured that he had Early exactly where he wanted him—caught between the main Federal army and Torbert's cavalry, which by then should have crossed New Market Gap. But soon Sheridan got two nasty surprises. First came word about Torbert: "I was astonished and chagrined," Sheridan wrote later, "to receive the intelligence that he had fallen back to Front Royal." It turned out that Torbert had been bluffed out of the Luray Valley by a force of Confederate horsemen half the size of his own cavalry.

Given Torbert's failure, Averell's division would have to redouble the speed of its pursuit. But Averell could not be found. Not until noon did his troopers trot into Wood-

In the engraving below of the battle at Fisher's Hill, Averell's cavalry at left and center drives Confederates from their entrenchments toward the distant Confederate artillery emplacements, while troops under Crook advance at right. Confederate Colonel Alexander S. (Sandie) Pendleton (*inset*), Early's chief of staff, was mortally wounded in the fighting.

stock. Incredibly, Averell had gone into camp at Fisher's Hill the previous evening, leaving the pursuit of the fleeing Confederates to the infantry. His career ended that afternoon. Furious, Sheridan forthwith ordered Colonel William H. Powell to take command of the 1st Cavalry Division.

Try as he might, Sheridan could not bring Early to bay. The Federal army continued south to Harrisonburg while the Confederates marched south to Port Republic and on up into the Blue Ridge Mountains. There Early began to receive reinforcements — Kershaw's footsore infantry division, shuttling over the mountains one more time; an artillery battalion; and later a brigade of cavalry under Brigadier General Thomas L. Rosser. But the string of defeats had demor-

alized Early's men. A dejected Georgia private wrote that his comrades in the mountain redoubt "seemed badly discouraged and looked like they thought it was useless to fight any longer."

With the reinforcements, Lee sent Early a grim message. "It will require the greatest watchfulness, the greatest promptness, and the most untiring energy on your part to arrest the progress of the enemy in the present tide of success. I have given you all I can."

On the outskirts of Petersburg, Grant had the Army of the Potomac's artillery fire a 100-gun salute to Sheridan's victory; Secretary of War Stanton ordered 15 commanders across the country to follow suit. "Keep on," Grant wired Sheridan, "and your good work will cause the fall of Richmond."

Hard Men Who Fought for Sheridan

Few armies of the Civil War included such an odd variety of units as the force Philip Sheridan was supposed to lead triumphantly up the Shenandoah Valley. The nucleus of Sheridan's command was General George Crook's Army of West Virginia — also known as VIII Corps — a motley collection of Shenandoah veterans that Crook himself called "little more than a large raiding party."

Contrasting with these rustic mountaineers were the disciplined troops of Major General Horatio Wright's VI Corps, recently detached from the Army of the Potomac. Despite heavy losses, they had displayed steady behavior in every crisis under Grant. Then there was XIX Corps, whose troops had endured the hard fighting and horrible climate of the Red River Campaign — and were delighted to be transferred north to the Shenandoah. Adding dash to the army was the Cavalry Corps, imbued with daring by Sheridan. "No finer body of 10,000 sabers could be found on this planet," bragged one trooper. Of the army's fiery leader, one infantryman said simply: "We all absolutely believed that Sheridan was invincible."

Portraits of the men, from privates to colonels, of this heterogeneous but hard-hitting force appear here and on the following pages with their corps banners.

VIII Corps

SERGEANT JOSEPH PECK
54TH PENNSYLVANIA

COLONEL GEORGE D. WELLS
34TH MASSACHUSETTS

COLOR GUARD OF THE 23RD OHIO

**COLONEL J. HOWARD KITCHING
PROVISIONAL DIVISION**

**LIEUTENANT FRANKLIN O.
SHERMAN, 10TH NEW YORK
HEAVY ARTILLERY**

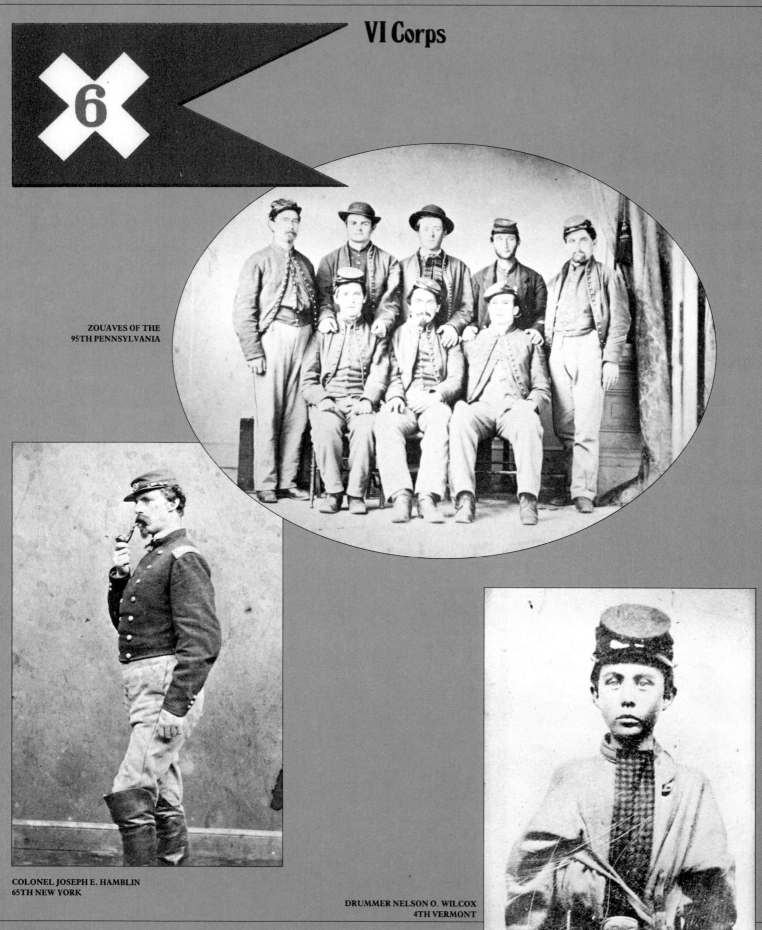

VI Corps

ZOUAVES OF THE
95TH PENNSYLVANIA

COLONEL JOSEPH E. HAMBLIN
65TH NEW YORK

DRUMMER NELSON O. WILCOX
4TH VERMONT

GENERAL J. WARREN KEIFER
AND STAFF

UNIDENTIFIED PRIVATE
151ST NEW YORK

XIX Corps

ZOUAVES OF THE
165TH NEW YORK

CHAPLAIN GEORGE KNOX
29TH MAINE

CAPTAINS JAMES FITTS AND
H.S. WHEELER, 114TH NEW YORK

SURGEON ISAAC SMITH, 26TH MASSACHUSETTS

COLONEL JOHN Q. WILDS,
24TH IOWA, AND OFFICERS

OFFICERS, 14TH PENNSYLVANIA CAVALRY

CAPTAIN MANNING D. BIRGE
6TH MICHIGAN CAVALRY

MAJOR HARVEY FARABEE
1ST WEST VIRGINIA CAVALRY

COLOR-BEARER
1ST CONNECTICUT CAVALRY

PRIVATE HENRY K. LANGDON
3RD MASSACHUSETTS CAVALRY

Showdown at Cedar Creek

"Never since the world was created was such a crushing defeat turned into such a splendid victory as at Cedar Creek."

CAPTAIN S. E. HOWARD, 8TH VERMONT

5 Generals Grant and Sheridan agreed that the Valley Campaign was over. They assumed that Early's demoralized army had fled across the Blue Ridge Mountains, probably to Charlottesville and perhaps as far as Richmond. The question now was what Sheridan should do next, and on that point the two generals disagreed.

The first sign of variance appeared in Sheridan's September 25 report to Grant from Harrisonburg. To the details of his movements since the fighting at Winchester and Fisher's Hill, Sheridan added a single unelaborated sentence: "I am now 94 miles from Martinsburg and 104 miles from Harpers Ferry." Sheridan knew his chief would not miss the significance of those distances to the nearest Federal railroad depots. As Grant was well aware, no large army could maintain itself for long, let alone engage in combat, when it depended for supplies on wagon trains plying a hundred miles of hostile country. Yet Grant could not forget that the Virginia Central Railroad was still in service to Lee's Army of Northern Virginia. "If you can possibly subsist your army to the front a few days more, do it," he urged, "and make a great effort to destroy the railroads about Charlottesville."

Sheridan thought this would be a mistake. Getting across the mountains would be difficult, and once there he would probably have to fight Early again. Meanwhile, his supply lines would be even longer. "I think the best policy," Sheridan told Grant, "will be

to let the burning of the crops in the Valley be the end of this campaign, and let some of this army go elsewhere." Grant bowed to Sheridan's judgment, at least for the moment, and gave him permission to withdraw as far as Strasburg.

Sheridan thus began a new and bitter phase of the Valley fighting, setting events in motion that would earn him both infamy and glory. For the manner in which he was about to make war on the countryside, Sheridan would create a legacy of hate among the residents of the Shenandoah. And for his conduct of the campaign's most dramatic battle, which was still to come, he would achieve his greatest fame.

For generations the residents of the upper Valley between Staunton and Strasburg would remember the autumn of 1864 as the time of "the Burning." Sheridan established the southern boundary of the devastation on September 26, when he sent his cavalry south to strip Staunton of all armaments, provisions and military equipment. The horsemen then moved eastward, tearing up the track of the Virginia Central all the way to Waynesboro. They were planning to destroy the iron railroad bridge and the tunnel through the Blue Ridge at Waynesboro. As they began the work, however, Early's entire force arrived from Brown's Gap and drove the Federal troopers back.

On the 29th, Sheridan ordered the cavalry to burn all the "forage, mills, and such other

Bullet holes and the bloodstains of Union and Confederate soldiers attest to the furious melee fought over the regimental colors of the 156th New York during the battle at Cedar Creek, Virginia, on October 19, 1864. In the space of 60 seconds the standard was lost and recovered three times, at a cost of two Confederate and three Federal lives. Afterward, a veteran of the regiment cut the eagle from the flag as a memento.

property as might be serviceable to the Rebel army" between Staunton and Harrisonburg. Military necessity or not, it was a distasteful business for many of the Federals who had to carry it out.

"What I saw there is burned into my memory," wrote Colonel James H. Kidd of Custer's brigade. Kidd's troopers had set fire to a mill in Port Republic, then turned back to help the village's residents save their homes from the flames. "The anguish pictured in their faces would have melted any heart not seared by the horrors and 'necessities' of war," Kidd wrote. "It was too much for me and at the first moment that duty would permit I hurried away from the scene." When the destruction had been accomplished as far north as Harrisonburg, Sheridan halted for a few days while he continued his correspondence with Grant about what the Army of the Shenandoah should do next.

During this lull, he suffered a bitter loss. On the evening of October 3, Sheridan's topographical engineer, 22-year-old Lieutenant John R. Meigs, son of the quartermaster general of the Union Army, was riding with two orderlies from Harrisonburg to Custer's headquarters, four miles to the southwest near Dayton. In a pelting thunderstorm, the three Federals overtook a small cavalry detachment trotting in the same direction.

All the riders were swathed in rubber ponchos and apparently were paying no attention to one another. But just as Meigs's party passed, the strangers whirled and fired, killing Meigs and one of the orderlies. The other was wounded, but he escaped to tell the tale. General Early later claimed it was a fair fight by Confederate cavalry scouts in uniform, who first demanded Meigs's surrender. But the Federals were outraged. "The whole thing was murder—no more, no less," declared Captain George B. Sanford of the 1st U.S. Cavalry.

In a fury, Sheridan ordered every house within five miles of Dayton burned to the ground. Artist James Taylor was at Sheridan's headquarters when the general gave the order to Custer. "Never shall I forget the dramatic episode," he recalled. "Custer vaulting into the saddle, and exclaiming as he dashed away, 'Look out for smoke!' " Soon, Taylor noted, "the ugly columns of smoke that rose in succession from the Valley like a funeral pall, told too well that he had fulfilled his orders to the letter."

But the harsh retaliation did not prevent Confederate bushwhackers from striking again. Just eight days after Meigs's death, Lieutenant Colonel Cornelius W. Tolles, Sheridan's chief quartermaster, and Dr. Emil Ohlenschlager, his medical inspector, were ambushed and mortally wounded.

The killings of Sheridan's aides were part of the ugly turn that the war in the Valley had taken after the Confederate defeats at Winchester and Fisher's Hill. The partisan rangers of John Mosby, Harry Gilmor and

Lieutenant John Roger Meigs, Sheridan's chief topographical engineer, is shot fatally in the back by a Confederate cavalryman on October 3, 1864. The killing provoked bitter controversy and so many conflicting stories that artist James E. Taylor sketched the Confederate version of the incident as well; it showed Meigs charging toward three Confederate scouts with his pistol drawn.

Hanse McNeill had bedeviled the Federals since the beginning of Sheridan's campaign, preying on supply lines and rear areas. The farther Sheridan intruded into the Valley, the more numerous and savage the attacks became. "No party of less than 50 men was safe a mile from camp," Captain Sanford asserted. "The loss in men, animals and supplies was enormous."

On the 25th of September, while General Alfred Torbert and his cavalrymen were returning from the Luray Valley, Lieutenant Charles McMaster of the 2nd U.S. Cavalry was mortally wounded near Front Royal in a clash with a band of Mosby's Rangers. McMaster's comrades insisted that he was robbed and then shot in cold blood after he had surrendered.

In retribution, the Federals summarily executed six Rangers who had fallen into their hands in the same engagement, shooting four of them and hanging the other two from a tree within sight of the town. Pinned to the chest of one of the victims was a note that read: "Such is the fate of all Mosby's gang." Within six weeks, a vengeful Mosby assembled a group of prisoners from Custer's Michigan brigade at his camp near Rectortown. He forced the men to draw lots to determine six of their number to be executed in retaliation for the Front Royal killings, and a seventh for the hanging of another partisan by Colonel William H. Powell. The condemned men were marched to a location as close as possible to Sheridan's headquarters and then hanged. But the Confederate squad bungled the executions — in some cases horribly. Three of the men were hauled to their tiptoes by the nooses and slowly strangled, two had to be shot and two somehow slipped away from their guards and escaped.

Mosby sent Sheridan a letter recounting both the Front Royal incident and his revenge, concluding with the threat: "Hereaf-

ter, any prisoners falling into my hands will be treated with the kindness due to their condition, unless some new act of barbarity shall compel me, reluctantly, to adopt a line of policy repugnant to humanity." Mercifully, there were no more such hangings, but the events created a pall of rancor over the Valley that was almost as tangible as the smoke from Sheridan's fires.

On October 5, immediately after Sheridan received Grant's approval to move north to Strasburg, a 20-mile line of blueclad riders spread out across the Valley, from North Mountain in the west to the Blue Ridge in the east. They put to the torch every conceivable source of food and comfort to the enemy — barns, granaries, haystacks and mills. William Averell's division, now under the command of Colonel Powell, worked down the Luray Valley on the east side of the Massanutten; Wesley Merritt's division was cen-

tered on the Valley Turnpike and extended to the Massanutten's western flank; and Custer — who had taken over James Wilson's division when the latter was sent west to a new command — moved on the right, between the pike and North Mountain. Their progress was marked by pillars of black smoke that darkened the sky.

Sheridan later reported the razing of 2,000 barns, 120 mills and half a million bushels of grain, and the confiscation of 50,000 head of livestock. Such demolition deprived civilians as well as Confederate soldiers of their subsistence. According to one official, many families were left "without a pound of meat, bread, or anything to live on, to say nothing of firewood."

The destruction enraged Jubal Early's army, which was not where the Federals thought it was. Instead of remaining at Waynesboro, it had marched back into the Valley. It took a position on the Valley pike halfway between Harrisonburg and Staunton on October 1, and made ready to attack Sheridan again.

One of Early's soldiers wrote that the march through a cold rain back to the Valley pike was "cruel and injudicious," since badly needed shoes and blankets were on the way to Waynesboro; on this and other grounds, Virginia Governor William Smith asked that Early be relieved and that his command be given to General Breckinridge. Lee refused, but he did mildly rebuke Early, observing: "You have operated more with divisions than with your concentrated strength. Circumstances may have rendered it necessary, but such a course is to be avoided if possible."

Unabashed, Early waited for a new cavalry commander — Brigadier General Thomas L. Rosser, who had been sent from Peters-

Brigadier General George A. Custer (*right foreground*) oversees his cavalry's withdrawal from Mount Jackson on October 7 and their destruction of forage and private property. "It was a severe measure," an officer reflected, "and appears severer now in the lapse of time, but it was necessary; the country was fruitful and was a paradise of bushwackers and guerrillas."

burg with his Laurel Brigade to take over for the wounded Fitzhugh Lee. The moment Rosser appeared, on October 5, Early prepared to attack, but by the next morning the Federals were on the move again. For the time being, the Confederates could only follow, angrily watching the Valley's abundance go up in smoke.

Spurred by their aggressive new commander, Rosser's cavalry snapped at the heels of Custer's barn-burners. Sheridan, professing himself "tired of these annoyances," summoned General Torbert to his headquarters and told his cavalry commander to start out at daylight and "whip the Rebel cavalry or get whipped."

At one time, it might have been foolhardy for Federal cavalry to attempt such a mission, so completely had Confederate horsemen dominated any field on which they rode. Here was the Laurel Brigade, which under the legendary Turner Ashby had consistently outfought the Federals; here were men who under Jeb Stuart had ridden around the entire Army of the Potomac. But all that was in the past. Ashby and Stuart were dead, as were most of the cavalry's blooded horses and many of the young men.

Torbert ordered Custer and Merritt to seek out the Confederate cavalry at dawn on October 9. The rival horsemen came face to face near Toms Brook along a five-mile line that stretched across the Valley from the Massanutten to the North Mountain. While the horse artillery of both sides blazed away, a line of dismounted Federal skirmishers advanced, followed by what a member of the Laurel Brigade called "moving masses of bluecoats, covering the hill slopes and blocking the roads with apparently countless squadrons." As Custer prepared to launch his attack, he spotted Rosser, an old friend and West Point classmate. Spurring his black horse ahead of the battle line, Custer doffed his hat in salute.

For two hours the lines charged and countercharged, the skirmishers dashing from position to position, the riders attacking batteries and firing their pistols and slashing at one another with their sabers. "In the center the Confederates maintained their position with much stubbornness," Sheridan recalled, "and for a time seemed to have recovered their former spirit."

But the Southerners had been worn out by their journey from Richmond and the constant fighting; and their infantry support was more than 20 miles away. At length Custer's troopers managed to turn Rosser's left flank. At the same time, Merritt launched two of his regiments in a thundering charge on the Confederate center, where Rosser's line connected with the division commanded by Major General Lunsford Lomax. "The result was a general smash-up of the entire Confederate line," wrote Sheridan, "the retreat quickly degenerating into a rout the likes of which was never before seen."

The Federals chased their beaten opponents for 26 miles, stopping only when they came up against Early's infantry at Rude's Hill just north of New Market. What was recorded officially as the Battle of Toms Brook became mockingly known, on both sides, as the Woodstock Races. But it was left to Jubal Early to make the unkindest cut of all: When he heard that the cavalry had let him down, he snarled of Rosser's brigade, "The laurel is a running vine."

Having routed the Confederates three times in three weeks, the Federals completed the destruction of the Valley as far north as they had been authorized to go. On October 10, they camped again along Cedar Creek, just north of Strasburg. Few of them suspected that the dogged Early was still on their heels, looking for a chance to even the score. When he learned from his spotters on Shenandoah Peak that VI Corps had left Sheridan's army to rejoin the Army of the Potomac, Early knew his chance had come; he marched northward on the Valley pike.

The Federal army was stationed across the mouth of the main Valley — the one to the west of Massanutten Mountain. The XIX Corps was massed near Belle Grove plantation, north of the Valley pike and a mile southwest of Middletown; General Crook's VIII Corps was camped east of the pike on a hill overlooking Cedar Creek. To the west, gently rolling farm country stretched to North Mountain, four miles away; a little more than two miles to the east, bordered by rugged, wooded hills, the broad Shenandoah flowed around the north end of Massanutten Mountain.

Early hoped to attack the Federal right, where he had plenty of room for maneuver and a chance to turn the enemy flank. But on October 13, before all of Early's troops were in place, Gordon's and Kershaw's divisions stumbled into battle with Crook's outposts on the Federal left. When Confederate artillery began shelling Crook's camp from atop Hupp's Hill, just northeast of Strasburg, Crook sent two brigades forward to develop the enemy position. Colonel George D. Wells's 1st Brigade became separated by a belt of woods and was counterattacked by seven regiments of South Carolinians under Brigadier General James Conner. The Federals were routed, losing 214 men to the Confederates' 182, and Wells himself fell mortal-

ly wounded. Despite this success, Early knew the Federals were now aware of his presence; he decided to withdraw to Fisher's Hill before attempting another advance.

Sheridan immediately recalled VI Corps, not only because of Early's startling aggressiveness but because the Federal high command was once more embroiled in a disagreement over strategy. Grant had again expressed the wish that Sheridan cut the Virginia Central Railroad at Gordonsville and Charlottesville. But chief of staff Halleck converted Grant's suggestion into an order, telling Sheridan to establish his army near Manassas Gap in the Blue Ridge and operate against the railroad from there. "This plan I would not indorse," Sheridan wrote bluntly in a later report.

Now Secretary of War Stanton got involved, and Halleck, having muddied the waters, called for a conference in Washington. Sheridan grudgingly complied, setting out for the capital on October 15, accompanied by his entire Cavalry Corps. The cavalry was to go with him as far as Front Royal, then head south to raid near Charlottesville. But when Sheridan reached Front Royal, he was shown an intercepted Confederate signal that gave him pause. The message, evidently from Richmond, was signed by the formidable Lieutenant General James Longstreet. "Be ready to move as soon as my forces join you," it read, "and we will crush Sheridan."

Sheridan suspected that the message was a ruse, as in fact it was — Jubal Early had written it and sent it to himself. He hoped that it would frighten Sheridan into retreating, thus giving the Confederates access to the food and forage that was still plentiful in the lower Valley. Instead, Sheridan called off the Charlottesville raid. Posting Powell's

Jubal Early's cavalry commanders — Brigadier General Thomas Rosser, Colonel Thomas Munford and Major General Lunsford Lomax *(left to right)* — undertook an expanded role in the Shenandoah Valley Campaign. The Confederate cavalry, despite its reduced size and the haggard condition of its mounts, served not only as Early's scouts, but also as a strike force to disrupt the flow of Federal supplies and counter the increasingly strong Union cavalry.

cavalry at Front Royal to guard against any approach by Longstreet from the Luray Valley, he sent the divisions of Merritt and Custer back to Cedar Creek. They carried a message for General Wright, who was commanding the army while Sheridan was gone. "Make your position strong," Sheridan told him. "Close in Colonel Powell. Look well to your ground, and be well prepared."

Early, unaware of Sheridan's absence, was almost ready to strike the Federal right. But on October 17, Gordon — "not entirely satisfied with the general plan of attack," he wrote later — climbed the rugged Shenandoah Peak to survey the situation. Gordon took with him three other officers, including Early's topographical engineer, Jed Hotchkiss. Through the crisp fall air, Gordon recalled, they could see not only "every road and habitation and hill and stream" for miles in every direction, but Sheridan's entire army as well — "every piece of artillery, every wagon and tent and supporting line of troops."

The three Federal corps were arrayed along the eastern bank of Cedar Creek, which for the final five miles of its course flows southeastward to its confluence with the North Fork of the Shenandoah. The Valley pike, running southwestward for the five miles from Middletown to Strasburg, crossed Cedar Creek at the midway point, the two features describing a gigantic X across the terrain.

Crook's VIII Corps was closest to the Confederates, with one division — Colonel Joseph Thoburn's — entrenched 1,000 yards north of the creek. The other two infantry corps were echeloned back to Crook's right, with William Emory's XIX Corps camped across the pike to the northwest and Wright's VI Corps next in line. Beyond the VI Corps's right, west of Middletown, were Merritt's and Custer's cavalry divisions. The Federals felt completely secure, and for good reason. With their 31,000 men they held a comfortable edge over the 21,000 Confederates opposing them.

The possibility of a sudden attack did occur to a few officers, including Captain Henry DuPont, whose guns were posted near Thoburn's division. DuPont wanted to know who was watching the wooded hills to the east. He was assured that Powell's cavalry division was on duty there, but when

A Proud Brigade's Outmoded Arms

The 600 men of the Laurel Brigade were rich in tradition but pinched for modern weapons when Brigadier General Thomas Rosser led them into the Shenandoah Valley early in October 1864. They were Turner Ashby's old Valley Cavalry — the 7th, 11th and 12th Virginia Regiments and Lieutenant Colonel Elijah White's 35th Virginia Battalion. Rosser rechristened them the Laurel Brigade

after the flowering shrub that abounded in the Valley.

The proud brigade suffered from the chronic shortage of efficient arms that plagued most of the Confederate cavalry. A few of its companies carried fast-firing Sharps carbines, but most of the troopers fought with obsolete muzzle-loaders like the two carbines shown below. Many used sawed-off shotguns,

which were effective only at very short range. Some companies had only revolvers — Colt and English Kerr models — to supplement their sabers.

By the time the Laurel Brigade withdrew from the Valley, after four months of hard fighting, it was completely outfitted with enemy Sharps, Spencer and Burnside breechloaders. But there were fewer than 300 men left to use them.

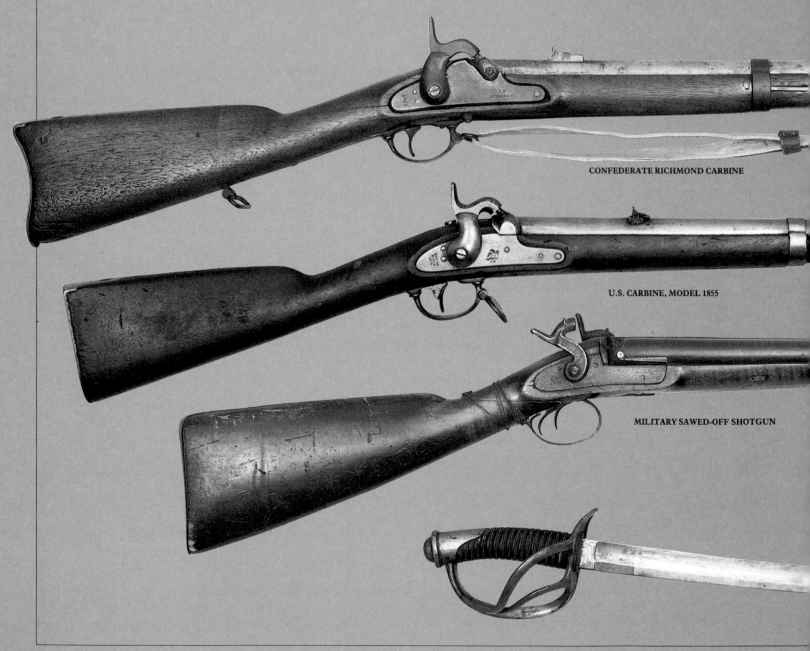

CONFEDERATE RICHMOND CARBINE

U.S. CARBINE, MODEL 1855

MILITARY SAWED-OFF SHOTGUN

ENGLISH KERR ARMY REVOLVER, MODEL 1859

The Laurel Brigade private below
wears a brigade badge on his hat like
the one at right, sent to Lieutenant
John R. Rust of the 12th Virginia by
his sweetheart in June 1864.

DRAGOON SABER, MODEL 1840

DuPont rode out to check, he found no one. In fact, only a single brigade of Powell's was in the area, and it was two miles downriver from the mouth of Cedar Creek. Apparently, Sheridan's instruction to "close in Powell" had been ignored.

From his mountain vantage point, General Gordon saw an enormous opportunity. If the Confederates could get through the thick woods, along the steep ridges and across the river, they could surprise and roll up the Federal left. And Gordon could see a road leading around the enemy flank — from a ford over the Shenandoah a half mile downstream from the mouth of Cedar Creek — that was guarded by a handful of cavalry pickets. Greatly excited, Gordon scrambled down to the Valley floor convinced he had found a way to destroy Sheridan's army.

Jubal Early was interested, but he thought that the plan lacked an essential element — a way to get to the ford. The next day, Gordon and Hotchkiss prowled the ravines and ridges at the foot of Massanutten Mountain until they found a trail leading through the woods around the Federal left.

That afternoon, Early issued orders setting the bold plan in motion. Gordon would attack the Federal left with three divisions while Early directed a two-division assault, supported by 40 guns, along the Valley pike against the center. The cavalry divisions would attack the flanks, Rosser to the west and Lomax circling to the east by way of Front Royal.

At nightfall that October 18, Gordon's men began the flanking movement. Stripped of anything that might rattle or clink, the Confederates crept silently along in single file. All night, Gordon recalled, "the long gray line like a great serpent glided noiselessly along the dim pathway." For a time, Gordon and Ramseur sat on a bluff and watched the men pass, Ramseur talking excitedly of the recent birth of his daughter. Married for almost a year, he was hoping for a victory so he could take leave and visit his wife and baby. When it was time to return to his duties, Ramseur stood up and said, "Well, General, I shall get my furlough today."

Long before dawn, Gordon's 7,000 men reached the ford across the Shenandoah, less than a mile from the exposed left of Sheridan's army. A couple of mounted Federal sentries sat their horses in midstream, unaware of the enemy soldiers hidden in the woods just yards away. Listening to the river and the restless shifting of the Federals' horses, Gordon waited tensely for the moment to attack.

A deepening chill that came with the first gray light of morning draped fog along the creek and river, sent it slowly spilling down the hollows and across the Valley floor. About 4:30 a.m., when he thought he could just make it to his assault position by 5 a.m., General Gordon ordered his men forward.

Colonel William H. Payne and 300 cavalrymen galloped firing into the river, sending the Federal sentries racing for camp. Payne's riders followed, under orders to strike toward Belle Grove and try to capture Sheridan himself. The main body of Federal troops heard the gunfire but discounted it; two cavalry reconnaissances in brigade strength were scheduled for that morning, and it was assumed the firing came from them.

Meanwhile, Kershaw's division had edged forward, just east of the pike, to the banks of Cedar Creek opposite Thoburn's camp. Early was with these troops, and he wrote later, "We got in sight of the enemy's fires at half-past three o'clock." The Confederates waited under cover of the woods until 4:30 a.m., then began crossing the creek and forming a line of battle. While doing so, they heard Gordon's encounter with the cavalry pickets. Then at precisely 5 a.m., by Early's recollection, they "swept over the enemy's left work, capturing seven guns, which were at once turned on the enemy." The surprise was complete. Kershaw's men were in Thoburn's camp before the Federals could get out of their tents.

At the same time, Rosser, with two cavalry brigades, attacked Custer's and Merritt's divisions on the Federal right. But the Federal cavalry was awake, under standing orders to be up before dawn when close to the enemy. And one of Merritt's brigades, commanded by Colonel Charles Russell Lowell,

was already in the saddle, preparing to make the scheduled reconnaissance. The Federal horsemen discovered Rosser's approach and stopped it cold.

Gordon's three divisions had hurried across the river, marching northward about a mile and passing east of Thoburn's position. When they reached the open fields of the Cooley farm, a half mile east of the camp of Crook's 2nd Division, they wheeled into a line of battle facing west, and howling the hair-raising Rebel yell, they charged.

General Clement Evans' Georgians swept over Thoburn's extreme left and rear almost immediately after Kershaw opened fire on the Federal front. Private G. W. Nichols of the 61st Georgia recalled that the Union soldiers "jumped up running and did not take time to put on their clothing, but fled

Dressed as farmers, General John Gordon (*foreground*) and Major Jedediah Hotchkiss, a topographical engineer, pretend to cut cornstalks in a field abutting a Federal outpost as they reconnoiter Sheridan's forces. "The entire Union army seemed but a stones throw away from us," wrote Gordon of the dangerous mission. "I could count, and did count, the number of Sheridan's guns."

With derisive cries of "Here's another Union victory!" Confederates
of Kershaw's division swarm into a
Federal camp in a surprise attack at
dawn on October 19, forcing the half-
asleep Federals to take up positions
on the outer side of their own rifle
pits. Colonel Joseph Thoburn (top),
whose unit was the first to be hit, died
while trying to rally his men.

in their night clothes, without their guns,
hats or shoes."

Captain DuPont managed to slow the
combined Confederate advance by firing
canister blindly into the fog, then he extricat-
ed two of his three batteries by conducting
the same kind of leapfrogging retreat he had
used at the Battle of New Market. Among
the many dead left on the field was Colonel
Thoburn, shot through the back while trying
in vain to re-form his division.

Crook's two divisions were widely separated. The 1st, temporarily commanded by
Colonel Rutherford B. Hayes in place of the
ailing General Isaac Duval, was a mile behind Thoburn's camp, across a wooded ravine. Alarmed by the heavy firing, Hayes
got his men up and was preparing to fight

when he was joined by Crook, Wright and
Emory. Not overly worried, the generals
helped Hayes form a line of battle behind his
camp, facing south. Emory brought two brigades from his corps to strengthen the right,
on the Valley pike; and Hayes bent his left
flank to the north to connect with the Provisional Division, recently attached to
Crook's command and led by Colonel J.
Howard Kitching.

Hayes rode over to check on the left and
was told by the 25-year-old Kitching, "I can
hold on here if you can hold on down there."
Miffed by the newcomer's airy response,
Hayes responded gruffly, "You need not feel
afraid for my line." As Hayes spoke, however, he looked back to the south and was confronted by an appalling sight.

Out of the fog — driving a disorganized throng of half-dressed stragglers before it — came a solid gray line of Confederates. These were Gordon's men, advancing from the east, not the south. The shock was too much for Kitching's troops. Even before contact was made, they began to withdraw. Kitching himself rode to the rear, his foot shattered by a bullet that would cause his death three months later. Hayes's men also gave way, at first in a trickle, then in a flood. Hayes's horse was killed under him and he avoided capture only by hiding in a grove of trees.

It was a strange retreat. The men were not frantic, remembered Captain S. E. Howard of XIX Corps, "only stolidly, doggedly determined to go to the rear." A few units here and there paused to shoot back, but Crook's command had come completely undone. "The broad plain was a scene of rout," one of Crook's staff officers recalled, "wagons, ambulances, artillery, soldiers without commanders, commanders without soldiers, every fellow for himself, moving backwards in sullen discouragement in the faces of the yelling victors."

The men of Emory's XIX Corps had more time to prepare for the onslaught, but they also had to contend with masses of fleeing VIII Corps soldiers and with an attack by all five of Early's divisions — General Wharton's men were coming into action now against Emory's right. Desperate for time to prepare his defenses, Emory sought out Colonel Stephen Thomas, who commanded a brigade made up of his own 8th Vermont, the 12th Connecticut and the 160th New York. Emory ordered Thomas to advance against the Confederate attackers. Thomas' brigade bravely crossed the pike and fired a volley. But the Federals had no time to re-load before the Confederates swarmed around them. "Men fought hand to hand," wrote Captain Howard of the 8th Vermont; "skulls were crushed with clubbed muskets; bayonets dripped with blood." A sea of Confederate hands reached out for the banners of the 8th Vermont, three color-bearers were killed, and "men actually clenched and rolled upon the ground in the desperate frenzy of the contest for the flags."

The Vermont regiment lost 110 of the 164 men engaged. "For a few moments," wrote Captain Herbert E. Hill, "the regiment was tossed about as a leaf in the small, fitful circle of a whirlwind, and then by a mighty gust lifted from the ground and swept from the field." Gordon's and Kershaw's victorious troops converged on the XIX Corps camp, flanking the protective earthworks and capturing several cannon and hundreds of prisoners.

By then General Wright had ordered XIX Corps to withdraw and re-form on the right of VI Corps. Emory retreated north past Belle Grove house, gathering fugitives from Crook's command and searching for a place to make a stand. Incongruously, Custer's divisional band, just a mile west of the pike, began to play a medley of tunes.

Torbert's cavalry had little trouble fending off Rosser's attacks on the right. As the signs of disaster multiplied on the left, Merritt wheeled his division to the southeast, extending it toward VI Corps, to face the enemy advance and try to halt the crowds of Federal stragglers. This the cavalrymen could not do, although they beat the fleeing men with their sabers and even opened fire on them. Torbert continued to shift the cavalry to the left, to hold the Valley pike and the fields to the east.

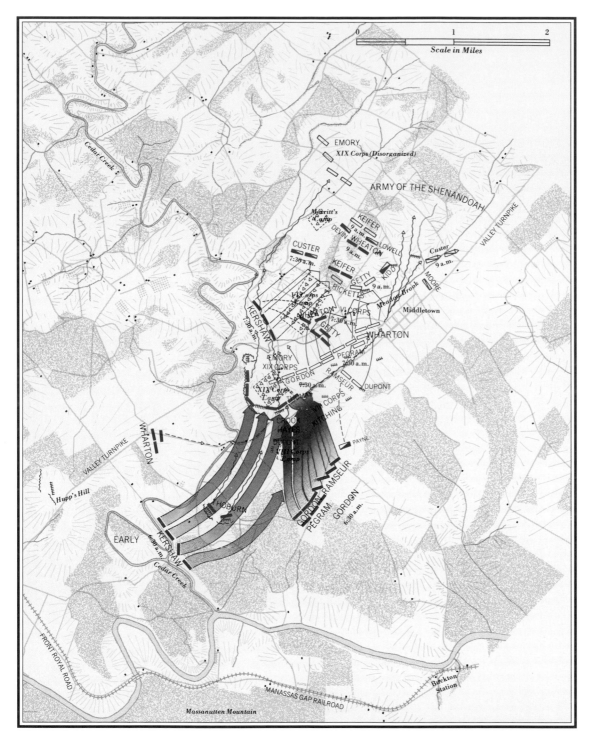

At 5 a.m. on October 19, Jubal Early launched a surprise attack on the Federal army camped between Cedar Creek and Middletown. Three Confederate divisions under John Gordon swept through the camps of George Crook's VIII Corps, and Joseph Kershaw's division routed Joseph Thoburn's two brigades. The Confederates pressed their advantage, driving XIX Corps from an entrenched position near Belle Grove plantation; but between 7 a.m. and 9 a.m. they were slowed by the dogged resistance of the Federal VI Corps. Philip Sheridan, absent when the battle began, arrived on the field at 10:30 a.m. and rallied his demoralized troops on a line north of Middletown.

As the rising sun began to burn the mists from the field, Early and Gordon met at Belle Grove. Early resumed direct control of Ramseur's and John Pegram's divisions; Gordon reverted to command of his own division — which had fought its way across the battlefield and was now on the Confederate left.

"We had captured nearly all of the Union artillery," claimed Gordon. "We had scattered in veriest rout two thirds of the Union army; while less than one third of the Confederate forces had been under fire, and that third was intact and jubilant." He admitted that the Federal VI Corps also remained intact, "but it was doomed unless some marvelous intervention should check the Confederate concentration which was forming against it."

Sixth Corps, temporarily under the command of General Ricketts, was the last to become engaged, as its camps were farthest from the point of attack. Even so, the men had barely stumbled into line before fugitives from the other corps came swarming past, pursued by exultant Confederates shouting what one Federal called "a yell like that of fiends." Ricketts deployed his 1st and 3rd Divisions on either side of the corps artillery and opened fire into the fog-shrouded ranks of Gordon and Kershaw. The Confederates wavered, but then Ricketts' 3rd Division gave way and Ricketts himself was carried wounded from the field. The 1st Division held off Ramseur for a time, then it too retreated, having lost half of its officers and a third of its men in less than 30 minutes. General Wright guided the withdrawal, blood dripping from a wound in his chin. The corps began to break up, brigades and sometimes regiments fighting on their own, but fighting hard.

Ricketts' successor, Brigadier General George W. Getty, had posted his 2nd Division in front of Middletown and now attempted to form a new line of defense with the survivors of the other divisions. No sooner had these men been herded into line than the storm broke, and the ranks went to pieces again. "As far down the line as could be seen in the fog," wrote Major Hazard Stevens of Getty's staff, "the men were breaking successively, file after file, like a row of toppling bricks set up in play by some sportive urchin." Realizing he was on his own, Getty pulled back across Meadow Brook and established a tight semicircular line on a ridge just west of Middletown. He deployed his remaining guns amid the gravestones of the town cemetery.

Here the battered remnants of VI Corps held on for nearly two hours against the repeated charges of Pegram, Ramseur and Wharton. Time after time the advancing ranks came within 30 paces of the Federal line before retreating down the corpse-strewn slope. Meanwhile, the shaken XIX Corps was re-forming behind the right flank of Getty's line while Crook tried to rally VIII Corps on the Valley pike behind Getty's left. Just east of the village, the cavalry was assembling, with Lowell's brigade in the lead, sparring with the Confederates for possession of the pike.

That morning, Colonel Lowell had lost the 13th horse to be shot from under him in as many weeks. But as his cavalrymen skirmished with Wharton's men, the colonel's legendary luck began to run out. A bullet slammed into Lowell's chest, failing to penetrate but striking with terrible force. Stunned, unable to speak and coughing blood, Lowell lay on the ground until it was time to lead his troopers again.

The Confederate attack was slowing and losing its cohesion. The stubborn resistance of VI Corps forced Early to shift his divisions and bring up his artillery; many of the Confederates left the ranks to plunder food and clothing from the Federal camps. "The smoking breakfast, just ready for the table, stood temptingly inviting," noted Captain Augustus Dickert of the 3rd South Carolina, "while the opened tents displayed a scene almost enchanting to the eyes of the Southern soldier, in the way of costly blankets, overcoats, dress uniforms, hats, caps, boots, and shoes all thrown in wild confusion over the face of the earth." Even a veteran officer like Dickert found the looting excusable. "All this fabulous wealth of provisions and

clothing looked to the half-fed, half-clothed Confederates like the wealth of the Indies."

The steadfast Getty continued to hold his position on the hill west of Middletown, but his men were running low on ammunition and were now raked by Confederate artillery fire. Again Pegram, Ramseur and Wharton led their men across Meadow Brook and up the bloody slope. This time four regiments of North Carolinians fought their way into the center of Getty's position, overrunning the guns of Battery M, 5th U.S. Artillery, despite salvos of double-shotted canister. "In a second they were amongst us," one gunner recalled, "amid smoke, fog, wreck, yells,

clash and confusion which no pen can depict and no pencil portray." Before the Confederates could exploit their breakthrough, Brigadier General Lewis Grant's Vermont Brigade charged to the aid of the artillerists, retaking the guns in savage fighting.

Brigadier General Daniel Bidwell's brigade pursued the Confederates to the banks of the creek before artillery fire killed Bidwell and scores of others. The survivors were driven back to the top of the hill. Getty decided that his men could not withstand another charge, and he drew back to a new defensive line a mile north of Middletown.

At midday the battle reached a fateful

As one color-bearer falls dead, the survivors of the 8th Vermont struggle at point-blank range to defend their flags against an onslaught of Confederate infantry at Cedar Creek. "The men realized they were in a terrible mess and fought like tigers," wrote one Vermonter. The unit "flung itself into the boiling cauldron where the fight for the colors was seething and dragged them out."

juncture. Early and Gordon would disagree long and bitterly over what happened next. Gordon believed that one more attack, made immediately, before the Federals could regain their balance, would win the day. But Early wanted to pause. "It was now apparent," he wrote in his official report, "that it would not do to push my troops further. They had been up all night and were much jaded."

Early was also concerned about the Federal cavalry, 7,500 strong, that was now massed beyond his right flank, east of the pike. Although Early had more than 5,000 horsemen himself, none of his units, with the exception of Payne's brigade, had made it to the main battlefield. Rosser's efforts had been repulsed with humiliating ease by Custer's division and Lomax was still off to the east. Thus the Federal horsemen rode the field unhindered by mounted opponents.

Early later claimed to have ordered one more advance by Gordon and Kershaw. According to Early, Kershaw replied that his men were ransacking the Federal camps and could not be formed in a line of battle. Gordon's division was also reported to be in such a state of disarray that the staff officer did not bother to give Gordon the order. A feeble advance was made nevertheless, but the Federals firmly repulsed it. Early decided, as he explained to Lee the next day, "to hold the advantages I had gained until all my troops had come up" — he was looking for Lomax — "and the captured property was secured."

Gordon, whose own official report on the battle mysteriously disappeared, later condemned Early's decision. Instead of attacking, said Gordon, "we halted, we hesitated, we dallied, firing a few shots here, attacking with a brigade or a division there. We waited, waited for weary hours," until the routed and disorganized Federals "had time to recover their normal composure and courage; waited till Confederate officers lost hope and the fires had gone out in the hearts of the privates."

The previous day in Washington, Sheridan had at last convinced Halleck and Stanton that instead of trying to operate against Charlottesville, he should retire to a defensible line in the lower Valley and send VI and XIX Corps back to Grant at Petersburg. Anxious to get back to his command, he took a special train to Martinsburg, then rode to Winchester with a 300-man cavalry escort. There, 15 miles from his Belle Grove headquarters, he spent the night.

Sheridan was awakened at 6 a.m. after a picket reported hearing the boom of distant artillery. Sheridan was not concerned, because he knew about the cavalry forays scheduled for that morning. But two hours later, when he had taken his breakfast and mounted up for the ride south, the firing had become "an unceasing roar." By the time he met his cavalry escort at a creek south of Winchester, he was certain that a battle was in progress and that his army was getting the worst of it. Worried now, Sheridan moved faster. "Just as we made the crest of the rise beyond the stream," he recalled, "there burst upon our view the appalling spectacle of a panic-stricken army — hundreds of slightly wounded men, throngs of others unhurt but thoroughly demoralized, and baggage wagons by the score, all pressing to the rear in hopeless confusion."

Sheridan barked orders for the posting of a brigade from Winchester across the pike to halt and reorganize the fleeing men. He selected Major George A. (Sandy) Forsyth and Captain Joseph O'Keeffe from his staff and 50 men from the 17th Pennsylvania Cavalry and, leaving the rest behind, increased his pace. Thus began one of the most famous rides in military history.

As the fiery little general on the big black gelding named Rienzi took the road to Cedar Creek at a rapid clip — not the flat-out gallop of legend and poetry — the fleeing men saw him, stopped, cheered, turned around and began to follow him toward the front. The effect of Sheridan's presence was remarkable; even Sheridan marveled at how quickly the mood of the men changed "from the depths of depression to the extreme of enthusiasm."

Sheridan later recalled telling the men, "If I had been with you this morning this disaster would not have happened. We must face the other way; we will go back and recover our camps." Sergeant L. L. Bell of the 110th Ohio remembered the general's words quite differently: "Come on back, boys! Give 'em hell, God damn 'em! We'll make coffee out of Cedar Creek tonight!"

Gradually Sheridan increased Rienzi's gait to a long, swinging lope, outdistancing all his escort except Forsyth, O'Keeffe and 20 troopers. The riders took to the fields to bypass the wagons and stragglers that clogged the road, Sheridan waving his cap to them and pointing to the front. "As he galloped on," recalled Major Forsyth, "his features gradually grew set, as though carved in stone, and the same dull red glint I had seen in his piercing black eyes when, on other occasions, the battle was going against us, was there now."

Sheridan reached the indomitable 2nd Di-

vision at 10:30 a.m. "Well, we've done the best we could," said the wounded General Wright. "That's all right," Sheridan responded kindly. But when General Emory rode over a minute later to report that a division of his corps was ready to cover the retreat to Winchester, Sheridan flared, "Retreat, hell! We'll be back in our camps

Sheridan gallops to rejoin his troops in this sketch of his dramatic ride, which shows him without the beard he wore at the time. "On he rode," remembered a VI Corps soldier, "his famous war-horse covered with foam and dirt, cheered at every step by men in whom new courage was now kindled."

tonight." Then he plunged into the work of re-forming the army.

Sheridan brought the other two VI Corps divisions and XIX Corps into line with Getty's 2nd Division, with XIX Corps on the right. He ordered Merritt's cavalry to remain on the army's left, but he moved Custer's to the right. Crook's men were gradually reassembling behind VI Corps as a reserve. After two hours Sheridan had established a solid line facing the now-hesitant Confederates.

Once his preparations were complete, Sheridan rode along his entire, two-mile front, cap in hand, showing himself to every soldier in the line. "I'll get a twist on these people yet," he yelled. "We'll raise them out of their boots before the day is over!" Major Walker recalled, "Cheers seemed to come from throats of brass, and caps were thrown to the tops of the scattering oaks." Although the men were eager to attack, Sheridan ordered them to lie down and wait. He was still concerned about the alleged approach of Longstreet's corps from Front Royal. Only when cavalry scouts assured him the report was untrue was Sheridan ready to make his move.

It was almost 4 p.m. An ominous silence fell over the field. "Even the batteries were still, recalled Colonel James H. Kidd, commanding Merritt's Michigan brigade. "The suspense was terrible." In the awful quiet the rival armies — 45,000 men in all — waited for the inevitable.

All along the line, the Federal infantrymen fidgeted nervously, retying their shoelaces, securing their pant legs inside their woolen socks, adjusting cartridge boxes and forage caps. "Then, almost as if by order," Major Forsyth recalled, "there rang from one end of the line to the other the rat-

tle of ramrods and snapping of gunlocks as each man tested for himself the condition of his rifle."

At last, Forsyth wrote, the order came: " 'Attention!' rings down the line. 'Shoulder arms! Forward! *March!*' And with martial tread and floating flags the line of battle is away." Confederate cannon erupted, Federal guns replied and musketry began to ripple down the lines.

"It was now life or death, and every man knew it," wrote Captain Hill of the 8th Vermont. The situation was especially perilous on the Federal right, where Colonel Thomas' decimated brigade had flung itself against Gordon's division. Custer rode off to the right to drive away Rosser's cavalry, with the result that the Federal infantry flank was overlapped by part of Evans' Georgia brigade. As Gordon's Confederates were forced back, stubbornly contesting every foot of ground, the Georgians laid a deadly enfilading fire at the Federal line.

Drawn to the point of crisis as always, Sheridan was there (on a fresh horse, renamed Breckinridge after the Confederate general, its former owner) to watch the brigade that had suffered so grievously in the morning take its revenge. On coming under fire from the right, Colonel Thomas' men drove away the Georgians who were beyond the Federal flank, then changed front and caught up with the fast-moving Federal line as it was executing a half-wheel to the left. In so doing, they punched through Evans' brigade and began to roll up Gordon's line. "This is all right!" shouted Sheridan enthusiastically, and galloped away to the left.

There VI Corps, supported by Merritt's cavalry and with Crook's reorganized VIII Corps in reserve, had begun to advance

Invigorated by Sheridan's return, the
Vermont Brigade forms for a counterattack at Cedar Creek as Confederate
prisoners *(left foreground)* are hustled
away in a painting by soldier Julian
Scott of Vermont. Sheridan admired
the work's accuracy, saying it "made
the boys as they were, going in."

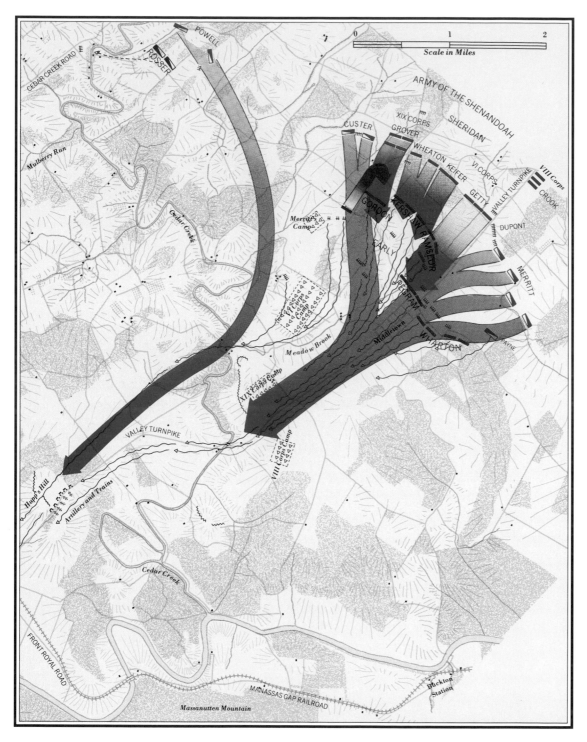

Shortly after 4 p.m. Sheridan counterattacked Early's forces with the reorganized troops of VI and XIX Corps. When Gordon's division on the Confederate left was flanked, Early's line began to crumble and soon was in retreat, despite a heroic stand by Ramseur's division. The onslaught of Federal cavalry under Custer and Merritt turned the retreat into a rout that continued until the Confederates halted four miles south of Cedar Creek. By nightfall, Sheridan's victory was complete.

down the Valley pike. Early had put all the strength he could muster against them, and Sheridan was trying to restrain his men in order to herd the Confederates eastward.

Merritt's horsemen got too far ahead of the infantry and ran into enfilading fire from the right. The wounded Colonel Lowell, waving his saber and whispering orders to an aide, was shot from his saddle by a bullet that severed his spine. "The cavalry once more fell back to the nearest ravine," wrote Colonel Kidd, "and whirling into line, without orders, was ready instantly for the last supreme effort."

The advance was soon resumed, Sheridan's infantry battling Confederates sheltered behind stone walls and impromptu breastworks of fence rails and earth. The

Confederate artillery fire was especially destructive. "More than half our killed and wounded were struck by shells," noted Private Lewis Bissell of the 2nd Connecticut Heavy Artillery. "They struck and burst in front, in the rear and among us. They plowed up the ground, covering us with dust and dirt." Bissell's hard-fighting brigade commander, Colonel Ranald Mackenzie, lost his second horse and received his third wound of the day while leading his men through the flying shrapnel.

But the Federal onslaught was unstoppable. The panic that had seized Gordon's men on the Confederate left began to spread along Early's entire line. Most of Kershaw's men took to their heels, "oblivious," reported one brigade commander, "of everything save to leave the enemy as far in the rear as possible." On the Confederate right, Wharton's division began to fall back before Merritt's cavalry, while Pegram's troops retreated through the streets of Middletown.

Ramseur's division, in the center, held on. The young commander, wearing a flower on his lapel in honor of his baby daughter, galloped up and down his line, keeping his men firmly in hand. Then, as the Federals pressed in from three sides, Ramseur's horse went down; he mounted another, which was also shot; he found a third and was preparing to mount when a rifle ball pierced both his lungs. His men carried their mortally wounded general to the rear as his line disintegrated.

The men of the 8th Vermont emerged from the woods to the west to watch the hasty Confederate withdrawal. Captain Hill remembered it as "a great, rushing, turbulent, retreating army, without line or apparent organization, hurrying and crowding on in mad retreat. Back across the sea of half-upturned faces of the enemy we could see the Union flags advancing amid the belt of smoke and flame that half encircled the doomed Confederates."

Across the seething battlefield, Federal cavalry bugles sounded the charge. "There came from the north side of the plain a dull, heavy, swelling sound," General Gordon wrote, "the omen of additional disaster." Merritt's horsemen on the left and Custer's on the right thundered toward the wavering Confederate flanks, the cheering infantry following close behind. As Major Forsyth put it, "Flesh that is born of woman could not stand such work as this." Early's army ceased fighting and thought only of escape.

Over Cedar Creek to Strasburg and beyond to Fisher's Hill the triumphant Federal cavalry galloped, gathering hundreds of prisoners, retaking the guns the Union had lost that morning and capturing 24 more.

They almost bagged General Gordon, but at the last moment he spurred his mount over a cliff at Fisher's Hill. The horse, Gordon wrote, "tumbled headlong in one direction, sending me in another." Briefly, man and beast lay unconscious, then both staggered to their feet. Gordon remounted and made his way to safety.

Near Strasburg, Federal troopers captured a wagon bearing the wounded General Ramseur. They took him to Belle Grove, where doctors could do nothing except ease his pain with doses of laudanum. During the evening several old friends from West Point — George Custer, Henry DuPont, Wesley Merritt — came to pay their respects. Ramseur died, wishing he could be with his wife on their first anniversary and see their newborn child.

A mile away in Middletown, Colonel Lowell lay paralyzed in a house that was crowded with wounded. He spent his last hours helping another young officer face death. "You were always brave," Lowell told him. "Now you must meet this as you have the other trials. Be steady. I count on you." Lowell died that night.

Early's army paused briefly at Fisher's Hill, then retreated all the way to New Market. In his report to Lee, Early wrote: "I found it impossible to rally the troops, they would not listen to entreaties, threats, or appeals of any kind. A terror of the enemy's cavalry had seized them. The rout was as thorough and disgraceful as ever happened to our army." Early insisted sourly that it was his men, not he, who had failed. But he added a paragraph showing that for all his vengeful sarcasm, he was capable of seeing himself in a clear light: "It is mortifying to me, General, to have to make these explanations of my reverses," he wrote. "They are due to no want of effort on my part, though it may be that I have not the capacity or judgement to prevent them. If you think that the interests of the service would be promoted by a change of commanders, I beg you will have no hesitation."

Lee did not relieve him then, but the Army of the Valley was finished as a fighting force. By Early's begrudging estimate, it had suffered almost 3,000 casualties—1,860 killed or wounded, 1,050 taken prisoner. The Confederates had inflicted 5,665 casualties, of whom 644 were killed and 3,430 wounded. But the Federals still had a numerical advantage of close to 2 to 1, and they now held complete sway over the devastated Valley.

The victory, and especially Sheridan's

Colonel Charles Russell Lowell, who was shot from his horse during the Federal counterattack at Cedar Creek, is shown here with his wife while on leave. In one of his last letters to her, Lowell shared a dire premonition: "I don't want to be shot until I've had a chance to come home," he wrote. "I have no idea that I shall be hit, but I *want* so much not to now, that it sometimes frightens me."

dramatic role, enraptured the North. Countless retellings of the story, and readings of Thomas Buchanan Read's poem "Sheridan's Ride," helped sweep away the feeling that the War could never be won; they contributed mightily to the reelection of President Lincoln. A grateful government rewarded Sheridan with permanent promotion to the rank of major general in the Regular Army.

The Valley Campaign was over. While Early's beaten army licked its wounds at New Market, sending Kershaw's division back to Lee, Sheridan's army went into winter quarters at Kernstown. During December, VI Corps rejoined the Army of the Potomac and Crook's VIII Corps was disbanded, Thoburn's old division joining Grant at Petersburg and Crook returning with the other division to West Virginia.

Back in the Valley, XIX Corps assumed garrison duty and Torbert led the cavalry on a raid across the Blue Ridge. On their return, the cavalrymen started hunting the partisans. They managed to capture only Harry Gilmor. Hanse McNeill was already dead, shot during a raid near Mount Jackson in

Confederate prisoners line up behind captured wagons and artillery in a sketch of Sheridan's Belle Grove headquarters at the close of the Battle of Cedar Creek. In all, the Federal victory yielded 1,200 prisoners, 115 wagons and ambulances, 1,600 rifles and 25 field pieces. This last figure left Sheridan incredulous until an aide assured him, "I've laid my hand on every one."

early October. But all efforts to destroy the legendary Mosby and his command failed, and he continued to plague Federal supply lines until the end of the War.

In February of 1865, Sheridan made his last advance up the Valley, with an infantry division and two divisions of cavalry under Merritt. Jubal Early made a defiant stand in front of Waynesboro on March 2, but Sheridan's advance regiments swept up nearly the entire force, capturing 1,600 men and 11 guns; Early and a remnant of his army made their escape.

Public opinion in Richmond was by now so inflamed against Early that Robert E. Lee was forced to relieve him of command. Now, the war as well as the campaign was over in the Shenandoah Valley. Sheridan's victorious army marched away for the last time, taking with it the rumble and clash of guns,

leaving behind a still-fertile Valley whose earth, warming in the spring sun, began to heal its scars.

Later in the spring of 1865 the VMI corps of cadets marched glumly west from Federally occupied Richmond to the burned-out ruin of their beloved institute at Lexington. It was soon rebuilt, and classes resumed; little had changed from the spring of 1864.

Henceforth, every May 15 at VMI, the roll call has included 10 additional names: those of the youths who died of wounds received at the Battle of New Market. As each name sounds across the parade ground—Cabell, Atwill, Crockett, Hartsfield, Haynes, Jefferson, Jones, McDowell, Stanard, Wheelwright—a specially honored cadet steps forward and responds: "Died on the field of honor, Sir!"

Witness to an Inspired Resurgence

At daybreak on October 19, as Jubal Early's Confederates lit into the Federals along Cedar Creek, the artist who would document the battle was in Winchester, 15 miles away. James E. Taylor (*self-portrait below, far right*)—a fervent Unionist who served two years with the 10th New York Zouaves before becoming an artist-correspondent for *Leslie's Illustrated Newspaper*—quickly responded to the sound of distant cannon fire. He hurried south, arriving in time to see the Federal recovery inspired by General Sheridan. After the War, Taylor drew on his notes and sketches, as well as on the sometimes highly flavored recollections of others, to produce an account of the Shenandoah fighting (*below*). Pictures from this work are shown here, with excerpts from Taylor's narrative of the Cedar Creek battle.

General Sheridan waves his cap to salute the men of the 3rd Division, VI Corps, identified by the Greek cross on their banner, in one of Taylor's most dramatic works.

As Taylor rode from Winchester to witness the fighting, he felt confident that Sheridan's Federal army was in command of the situation. But before covering half the distance to Cedar Creek, he came across disturbing evidence to the contrary.

"I had reached the edge of Kernstown when I encountered a squad of half clothed wild eyed panting Blue Coats hurrying in the direction of Winchester. Astonished at the spectacle, I made an effort to halt them to inquire the cause, but they paid no attention to me further than to shout as they whirled by: 'Our army is defeated and all cut to pieces.'"

Taylor hurried into Kernstown, "still doubtful that disaster could have befallen the invincible Sheridan." But hope vanished when, to the south, Taylor saw "swarming toward me in scattered disorder teams and soldiers, inextricably mingled. At sight of this ominous herald of calamity I could but feel that Sheridan had too met his Waterloo in this fateful Valley."

Pressing on against the current of the retreating Federals, Taylor reached Bartonville around 9:30 a.m. There the mood of the troops changed: "Down the road from the crowd of fugitives came murmurs like the breaking of a surge on a far off shore. Nearer it grew, grew louder and swelled to a tumult — cheers, the cheers of the stragglers.

"As I gazed I was seized with amazement to see the tide of the stragglers retracing their steps. Then suddenly from among them a horseman dashed into the field, followed by others. I recognized in the lead General Sheridan."

On the pike, Sheridan embraces General George Crook (left, under banner) while General Horatio Wright, hand in jacket, looks on.

Union cavalrymen of Brigadier General Wesley Merritt's division storm a
Confederate battery north of Middletown around 4 p.m.

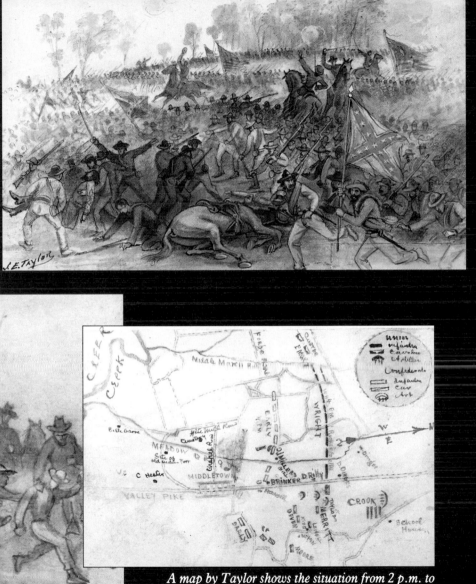

Troops of the Federal XIX Corps under Brigadier General William Emory repulse an assault on the Union right about 2 p.m.

A map by Taylor shows the situation from 2 p.m. to 4 p.m., when Sheridan ordered a final advance.

In the frenzy of Federal activity that followed Sheridan's arrival on the battlefield, Taylor was able to catch only fleeting glimpses of the events unfolding along the front. He labored diligently afterward to fill the gaps in his chronicle, evolving detailed illustrations and maps from the reports of eyewitnesses. One such source, an aide to General George Crook, furnished Taylor with a graphic account of the meeting that morning between Sheridan and two of his trusted subordinates.

"About 10 a.m. General Wright, in command during General Sheridan's absence, and General Crook were holding a council of war by the Pike. Suddenly a shout is heard, the cheers increasing, when General Sheridan appears on his black charger.

"He dismounted and approached Wright and Crook, exclaiming, 'What are you doing way back here?' He then threw his arms about General Crook.

"After the embrace of the two brave men I thought I saw moisture in the eyes of both. Sheridan then shook the hand of General Wright, and noticing some blood on his whiskers from where it had trickled down from a bullet wound in his chin, he said: 'Ah, ha! You're wounded.' 'Only a scratch,' said General Wright.

"After some minutes of conversation Sheridan remounted, and as he did so I heard him say: 'If I can get our men rallied again, we'll put them back a D— sight faster than they came.' "

It would be several hours, however, before Sheridan — having made certain that James Longstreet's large Confederate corps posed no threat — was ready to make good on his pledge. In the interim, the Federals beat back a final enemy thrust and launched probing attacks of their own.

J.E.TAYLOR

A midafternoon lull gave Taylor a chance to position himself to see the resumption of the fighting. B[...]he time Sheridan sent Wright's VI Corps forward about 4 p.m., the artist was looking on with sketchbook in hand from an excellent vantage point — the crest of a slope just 50 yards behind the Federal lines. He later described the advance:

"Now the Sixth Corps, with wild cheers, moved down the grape-swept slope amid dust and flying gravel and thinning ranks and up the corresponding grade to face the deadly musketry fire from behind the stone barricades and sheltering objects. Hark! above the roar of the artillery and musketry fire rises the battle shout of the charging infantry as they sweep over th[...]barriers despite the frantic efforts by the Confederates to hold their lines and stem the current of pursuit."

Of Sheridan's order to launch this drive, Taylor remarked in his journal: "It may have been said to sound the death knell of the Southern Confederacy, for it was the signal for the almost instant and total destruction of the last aggressive army in Virginia. Well we can exclaim: 'It required the magic of Sheridan's name and genius to transform such a defeat into victory.'"

Union Colonel Charles Lowell (mounted, center) is hit by sniper fire from the Brinker house.

Shot while attempting to rally his Confederates, General Stephen Ramseur collapses into the arms of an aide.

Sheridan summons the men of Crook's corps to join in the attack.

Troopers of Brigadier General George A. Custer's 3rd Cavalry Division assail the retreating Confederate infantrymen on Hupp's Hill.

In the closing stages of the Battle of Cedar Creek, men on horseback played a dramatic part — a point not lost on the watchful Taylor. As a soldier and artist, he had a deep appreciation for the inspirational effect of a bold charge by masses of cavalry — or a valiant gesture by a single mounted officer — and he dwelt lovingly on such moments in his chronicle of the event.

To depict the mortal woundings of Union Colonel Charles Russell Lowell and Confederate Major General Stephen Ramseur, Taylor relied on the observations of others. But for his portrait of Sheridan mounted on his black charger and urging on Crook's corps, the artist was his own primary source: He was with Crook's men as they waited in reserve behind Wright's corps, hoping for a chance to redeem themselves after their sorry performance earlier in the day. As Taylor relates, that opportunity was not long in coming:

"While I was absorbed in the thrilling spectacle of the Sixth Corps charge, a sound like to a distant cheer greeted me, which grew in volume. Like an apparition Sheridan burst on Crook's front, as if from the earth risen. Aloft he swings his cap as his strong harsh voice fairly shrieks: 'Forward boys! Follow me! We'll sleep in the old camp tonight!'

"The responsive shout from the enthusiastic Blue Coats was like a thunder peal, for there was no resisting the magnetism of the man."

Soon the Confederates gave way, and the opportunistic General George Custer took up the chase. "Custer was in the van with his cavalry," Taylor notes. "On Hupp's Hill he struck Early's infantry and made his first big haul in his headlong reckless charge among the foot soldiers, sabering right and left."

167

Although he was drawn to the heroic, Taylor was by no means blind to the moments of confusion and panic that punctuated the Battle of Cedar Creek — a conflict that began with one army on the run and ended with the other in panicky retreat. The last battle scene in Taylor's sequence captures the desperate effort of Jubal Early's rear elements to elude the pursuing Federal cavalry along the turnpike. The artist, who relied in this instance on the accounts of participants, later elaborated on the situation in his journal:

"At the upper end of Strasburg, Merritt united with Custer to harass the flank of the retreating column. A half mile from the town at the little stream that pours down the hill and crosses the road neath a bridge, our sharpshooters killed some artillery horses, which falling on the structure clogged the way, and the road became at once blocked with guns, caissons, ambulances, and wagons. Custer and Devin swooping upon these gathered them up, for the disorganized mob took to the field, neither attempting to check the pursuit nor attempting to save anything.

"At the bridge over Tumbling Run for prudential reasons the pursuit of Custer and Devin ended. In the 'Pocket' by this bridge a large number of prisoners were taken as the broken-down caisson prevented the enemy's stragglers utilizing the only avenue to safety."

Custer comforts the dying Ramseur during a midnight vigil at the Belle Grove house.

Operating in Middletown's Episcopal Church on October 20, a surgeon amputates the leg of a trooper as stretcher-bearers bring in another casualty.

Fresh from seizing the Confederate guns at Tumbling Run, an excited Custer lifts Sheridan from the ground.

Around 9 p.m., Custer returned in triumph from Tumbling Run to Sheridan's camp near the Belle Grove estate. Taylor later recalled the moment:

"As Sheridan saw Custer approaching, there being a great log fire by the tents to light the darkness, he walked out to meet him and while yet several feet away he said: 'You have done it for me this time, Custer.' And then as 'Yellow Hair' came up, Sheridan caught hold of him and pulled him off his horse, when Custer seizing Sheridan around the waist lifted him high up and in wild glee danced and whirled him around and round, completely lost to military deportment in his intoxicating joy, exclaiming as their tears mingled: 'By G— Phil, we've cleaned them out of their guns and got ours back.'"

Like the generals, Taylor reveled in the victory. But his elation was soon tempered by a realization of the price both sides had paid, and he added two sobering postscripts to his account: a view of Custer at Ramseur's deathbed and a sketch of a church the Federals had turned into a hospital. Witnessing the grim services performed there, Taylor learned the limits of his curiosity.

"Among the soldiers being repaired were some Blue Coats that had been wounded in the morning's surprise in this vicinity. A Federal surgeon was doing the operating. As I made my last crayon stroke he was in the act of amputating a limb of a stalwart cavalryman, but I did not stop to see the repulsive sight and hurried out. In the church yard was a mass of maimed soldiers, mostly the Gray, who had been cut, sawed and more or less mutilated in the haphazard work of the surgeons necessitated by the occasion— with wounds bound up, stretched in rows, all bloodless and pale."

ACKNOWLEDGMENTS

The editors wish to thank the following individuals and institutions for their valuable assistance in the preparation of this volume:

Illinois: Chicago — Richard Tibbals.

Maryland: Hagerstown — Douglas Bast, Washington County Historical Society.

New York: Latham — Camille O'Leary, State of New York, Division of Military & Naval Affairs. Lyons — Charles E. Ennis. Olivebridge — Seward R. Osborne.

Ohio: Cleveland — Ann K. Lindelar, Western Reserve Historical Society. Columbus — Larry M. Strayer.

Pennsylvania: Carlisle — Randy Hackenburg, Michael J. Winey, U.S. Army Military History Institute. Chambersburg — Lillian Colletta, Kittochtinny Historical Society Library. Greencastle — Ted Alexander. Harrisburg — Richard A. Sauers, Pennsylvania Capitol Preservation Committee. Pittsburgh — Al Richardson.

Vermont: Springfield — Nick Picerno.

Virginia: Alexandria — Col. Robert B. Ennis. Fredericksburg — Robert K. Krick, Fredericksburg-Spotsylvania National Military Park. Front Royal — Lola Wood, Warren Rifles Confederate Museum. Lexington — June F. Cunningham, Diane Jacob, Tom Joynes, Brig. General John W. Knapp, Julia Smith Martin, Virginia Military Institute. Lynchburg — Patricia A. Hobbs, Lynchburg Museum System. New Market — Frances Good, Robert S. Myers, New Market Battlefield Park. Richmond — Charlene S. Alling, David C. Hahn, Museum of the Confederacy; Linda Leazer, Virginia Historical Society.

The index for this volume was prepared by Roy Nanovic.

BIBLIOGRAPHY

Books

Bean, W. G., *Stonewall's Man: Sandie Pendleton.* Chapel Hill: The University of North Carolina Press, 1959.

Bellard, Alfred, *Gone for a Soldier: The Civil War Memoirs of Private Alfred Bellard.* Ed. by David Herbert Donald. Boston: Little, Brown and Co., 1975.

Beyer, W. F., and O. F. Keydel, eds., *Deeds of Valor from Records in the Archives of the United States Government.* Vol. 1. Detroit: The Perrien-Keydel Co., 1906.

Blackford, Charles M., *Campaign and Battle of Lynchburg, Va.* Lynchburg: J. P. Bell Co., 1901.

Boatner, Mark Mayo, III, *The Civil War Dictionary.* New York: David McKay Co., 1959.

Buell, Augustus, *"The Cannoneer." Recollections of Service in the Army of the Potomac.* Washington, D.C.: The National Tribune, 1890.

Burr, Frank A., and Richard J. Hinton, *The Life of Gen. Philip H. Sheridan.* Providence: J. A. & R. A. Reid, 1888.

Carpenter, George N., *History of the Eighth Regiment Vermont Volunteers, 1861-1865.* Boston: Press of Deland & Barta, 1886.

Catton, Bruce, *Grant Takes Command.* Boston: Little, Brown and Co., 1969.

Clark, Walter, ed., *Histories of the Several Regiments and Battalions from North Carolina in the Great War 1861-'65.* Vols. 2 and 3. Wendell, N.C.: Broadfoot's Bookmark, 1982 (reprint of 1901 edition).

Cohen, Stan, *The Civil War in West Virginia: A Pictorial History.* Charleston, W. Va.: Pictorial Histories Publishing Co., 1982.

Cooling, Benjamin Franklin, *Symbol, Sword, and Shield.* Hamden, Conn.: The Shoe String Press, 1975.

Couper, William, *One Hundred Years at V.M.I.* 4 vols. Richmond: Garrett and Massie, 1939.

Crook, George, *General George Crook: His Autobiography.* Ed. by Martin F. Schmitt. Norman: University of Oklahoma Press, 1960.

Davis, William C.:
The Battle of New Market. Garden City, N.Y.: Doubleday & Co., 1975.
Breckinridge: Statesman, Soldier, Symbol. Baton Rouge: Louisiana State University Press, 1974.

De Forest, John William, *A Volunteer's Adventures: A Union Captain's Record of the Civil War.* Ed. by James H. Croushore. New Haven, Conn.: Yale University Press, 1946.

Dickert, D. Augustus, *History of Kershaw's Brigade.* Dayton: Morningside Bookshop, 1976.

Early, Jubal Anderson, *War Memoirs.* Ed. by Frank E. Vandiver. Bloomington: Indiana University Press, 1960.

Eby, Cecil D., Jr., *"Porte Crayon": The Life of David Hunter Strother.* Chapel Hill: The University of North Carolina Press, 1960.

Elting, John R., and Michael J. McAfee, eds., *Long Endure: The Civil War Period, 1852-1867.* Vol. 3 of *Military Uniforms in America.* Novato, Calif.: Presidio Press, 1982.

Emerson, Edward W., *Life and Letters of Charles Russell Lowell.* Boston: Houghton, Mifflin and Co., 1907.

Fisk, Wilbur, *Anti-Rebel: The Civil War Letters of Wilbur Fisk.* Croton-on-Hudson, N.Y.: Emil Rosenblatt, 1983.

Flinn, Frank M., *Campaigning with Banks in Louisiana, '63 and '64, and with Sheridan in the Shenandoah Valley in '64 and '65.* Boston: W. B. Clarke & Co., 1889.

Forsyth, George A., *Thrilling Days in Army Life.* New York: Harper & Brothers, 1900.

Freeman, Douglas Southall, *Gettysburg to Appomattox.* Vol. 3 of *Lee's Lieutenants: A Study in Command.* New York: Charles Scribner's Sons, 1944.

Gallagher, Gary W., *Stephen Dodson Ramseur: Lee's Gallant General.* Chapel Hill: The University of North Carolina Press, 1985.

Gordon, John B., *Reminiscences of the Civil War.* New York: Charles Scribner's Sons, 1903.

The Hagerstown Bank at Hagerstown, Maryland: Annals of 100 Years, 1807-1907. New York: The Knickerbocker Press, 1910.

Hattaway, Herman, and Archer Jones, *How the North Won: A Military History of the Civil War.* Urbana: University of Illinois Press, 1983.

Hoke, J., *Reminiscences of the War; or Incidents Which Transpired in and about Chambersburg, during the War of the Rebellion.* Chambersburg, Pa.: M. A. Foltz, 1884.

Hotchkiss, Jedediah, *Make Me a Map of the Valley: The Civil War Journal of Stonewall Jackson's Topographer.* Ed. by Archie P. McDonald. Dallas: Southern Methodist University Press, 1973.

Johnson, Robert Underwood, and Clarence Clough Buel, eds., *Battles and Leaders of the Civil War.* Vol. 4. New York: The Century Co., 1887.

Kidd, J. H., *Personal Recollections of a Cavalryman.* Ionia, Mich.: Sentinel Printing Co., 1983 (reprint of 1908 edition).

Kitching, J. Howard, *"More than Conqueror," or Memorials of Col. J. Howard Kitching, Sixth New York Artillery, Army of the Potomac.* New York: Hurd and Houghton, 1873.

Leech, Margaret, *Reveille in Washington 1860-1865.* New York: Harper & Brothers, 1941.

Lincoln, William S., *Life with the Thirty-Fourth Mass. Infantry in the War of the Rebellion.* Worcester, Mass.: Noyes, Snow & Co., 1879.

Longacre, Edward G., *From Union Stars to Top Hat: A Biography of the Extraordinary General James Harrison Wilson.* Harrisburg, Pa.: Stackpole Books, 1972.

Military Historical Society of Massachusetts, *The Shenandoah Campaigns of 1862 and 1864 and the Appomattox Campaigns of 1865.* Vol. 6 of *Papers of the Military Historical Society of Massachusetts.* Boston: The Military Historical Society of Massachusetts, 1907.

Military Order of the Loyal Legion of the United States, Indiana Commandery, *War Papers Read before the Indiana Commandery.* Indianapolis: The Commandery, 1898.

Military Order of the Loyal Legion of the United States, Massachusetts Commandery, *Civil War Papers.* Vol. 2. Boston: Printed for the Commandery, no date.

Morsberger, Robert E., and Katharine M. Morsberger, *Lew Wallace: Militant Romantic.* New York: McGraw-Hill Book Co., 1980.

Mosby, John S., *The Memoirs of Colonel John S. Mosby.* Ed. by Charles Wells Russell. Millwood, N.Y.: Kraus, 1981.

Mowrer, G. H., comp., *History of the Organization and Service during the War of the Rebellion of Co. A, 14th Pennsylvania Cavalry.* Pittsburgh: Art Engraving & Printing Co., no date.

Nichols, G. W., *A Soldier's Story of His Regiment (61st Georgia).* Kennesaw, Ga.: Continental Book Co., 1961.

Olcott, Mark, with David Lear, *The Civil War Letters of Lewis Bissell.* Washington, D.C.: The Field School Educational Foundation Press, 1981.

Slease, William Davis, *The Fourteenth Pennsylvania Cavalry in the Civil War.* Pittsburgh: Art & Engraving Co., 1915.

Stackpole, Edward J., *Sheridan in the Shenandoah: Jubal Early's Nemesis.* Harrisburg, Pa.: The Stackpole Co., 1961.

Starr, Stephen Z., *From Fort Sumter to Gettysburg 1861-1863.* Vol. 1 in *The Union Cavalry in the Civil War.* Baton Rouge: Louisiana State University Press, 1979.

Strother, David Hunter, *A Virginia Yankee in the Civil War: The Diaries of David Hunter Strother.* Ed. by Cecil D. Eby Jr. Chapel Hill: The University of North Carolina Press, 1961.

Swinfen, David B., *Ruggles' Regiment: The 122nd New York Volunteers in the American Civil War.* Hanover, N.H.: University Press of New England, 1982.

Turner, Edward Raymond, *The New Market Campaign: May, 1864.* Richmond: Whittet & Shepperson, 1912.

United States War Department, *The War of the Rebellion.* Series 1 — Vol. 37, Part 2, Additions and Corrections. Vol. 40, Part 3. Vol. 43, Additions and Corrections. Washington, D.C.: Government Printing Office, 1891-1902.

Vaill, Dudley Landon:
The County Regiment: A Sketch of the Second Regiment of Connecticut Volunteer Heavy Artillery, Originally the Nineteenth Volunteer Infantry, in the Civil War. Litchfield County, Mass.: University Club, 1908.
History of the Second Connecticut Volunteer Heavy Artillery. Winsted, Conn.: Winsted Printing Co., 1868.

Walker, Aldace F., *The Vermont Brigade in the Shenandoah*

Valley, 1864. Burlington, Vt.: The Free Press Association, 1809.

Williams, T. Harry, *Hayes of the Twenty-Third: The Civil War Volunteer Officer*. New York: Alfred A. Knopf, 1965.

Williamson, James J., *Mosby's Rangers*. New York: Ralph B. Kenyon, 1896.

Wilson, James Harrison, *Under the Old Flag*. Vol. 1. Westport, Conn.: Greenwood Press, 1971.

Wise, Jennings Cropper, *The Long Arm of Lee: The History of the Artillery of the Army of Northern Virginia*. New York: Oxford University Press, 1959.

Wise, John Sergeant, *The End of an Era*. Ed. by Curtis Carroll Davis. New York: Thomas Yoseloff, 1965.

Worsham, John H., *One of Jackson's Foot Cavalry*. Ed. by James I. Robertson Jr. Jackson, Tenn.: McCowat-Mercer Press, 1964.

Worthington, Glenn H., *Fighting for Time*. Shippensburg, Pa.: Beidel Printing House, 1985.

Other Sources

Alexander, Ted, "Retaliation in Kind." Unpublished article.

Bilby, Joseph:

" 'Every damn . . . rebel is on the run!' " *Military Images Magazine*, November-December 1980.

"9 July 1864: The 14th New Jersey Infantry at the Battle of Monocacy." *Military Images Magazine*, May-June 1980.

"Gen. M'Causland in Chambersburg!" *The Old Flag*, Chambersburg, Pa., August 25, 1864.

" 'Grumble' Jones: A Personality Profile." *Civil War Times Illustrated*, June 1968.

Johnson, Bradley Tyler, "My Ride around Baltimore in Eighteen Hundred and Sixty-Four." *Journal of the United States Cavalry Association*, 1889.

Kimball, William J., "The Battle of Piedmont." *Civil War Times Illustrated*, January 1967.

Langellier, John Phillip, and Wayne Colwell, "Cavaliers from California." *Gateway Heritage*, winter 1984-1985.

Pohanka, Brian, "The Battle of Monocacy." Unpublished paper, 1972.

Smith, Harold F., "Mulligan and the Irish Brigade." *Journal of the Illinois State Historical Society*, summer 1963.

Stinson, Byron, "The Invalid Corps." *Civil War Times Illustrated*, May 1971.

Taylor, James E.:

"War Correspondent: 1864." *American Heritage*, August-September 1980.

"With Sheridan Up the Shenandoah Valley in 1864: Leaves from a Special Artists Sketch Book and Diary." Unpublished manuscript.

Tibbals, Richard K.:

" 'Go East, Young Man . . .' " *Military Images Magazine*, May-June 1984.

"Thirty Years Later." *Civil War Times Illustrated*, April 1986.

Wert, Jeffrey, " 'Little Phil' Makes a Shambles of the Shenandoah Valley." *Civil War Times Illustrated*, May 1980.

PICTURE CREDITS

Credits from left to right are separated by semicolons, from top to bottom by dashes.

Cover: Painting by Thure de Thulstrup, Seventh Regiment Fund Inc., photographed by Al Freni. 2, 3: Maps by Peter McGinn. 8, 9: Inset courtesy Virginia Military Institute (VMI) Archives, Lexington; Washington and Lee University, both photographed by Michael Latil. 10, 11: Paintings by William C. Brown; Adele Williams; and William D. Washington, VMI Museum, Lexington — VMI Museum, Lexington; VMI Archives, Lexington; inset, VMI Museum, Lexington, all photographed by Michael Latil. 12: VMI Museum, Lexington, photographed by Michael Latil, except top left portrait attributed to photographer Samuel Pettigrew courtesy Stonewall Jackson House Collection, Historic Lexington Foundation, copied by Thomas C. Bradshaw. 13: VMI Archives, Lexington, all copied and photographed by Michael Latil. 14: VMI Archives, Lexington, copied by Michael Latil. 15: Painting by John P. Walker, Jackson Memorial Hall, VMI, Lexington; Valentine Museum, Richmond; VMI Archives, Lexington, copied by Michael Latil(5). 17: New Market Battlefield Park, Hall of Valor Museum, photographed by Michael Latil. 18: Painting by E. F. Andrews, Kentucky Museum, Western Kentucky University, Bowling Green, photographed by Bill LaFevor. 21: Massachusetts Commandery of the Military Order of the Loyal Legion of the United States and the U.S. Army Military History Institute (MASS-MOLLUS/USAMHI), copied by A. Pierce Bounds — National Archives Neg. No. 111-B-4691. 22: R. B. Hayes Presidential Center, HN#553 — sketch by J. W. Oswald, R. B. Hayes Presidential Center, HN#724. 23: National Archives Neg. No. 111-BA-1218. 24: National Archives Neg. No. 111-B-6144. 25: Courtesy of The Cincinnati Historical Society. 26, 27: MASS-MOLLUS/USAMHI, copied by A. Pierce Bounds. 29: Painting by William Sheppard, Museum of the Confederacy, Richmond, photographed by Katherine Wetzel. 31: MASS-MOLLUS/USAMHI, copied by A. Pierce Bounds. 32: VMI Museum, Lexington, photographed by Michael Latil. 33: New Market Battlefield Park, Hall of Valor Museum, photographed by Michael Latil. 35: Painting by Benjamin West Clinedinst, Jackson Memorial Hall, VMI, Lexington, photographed by Michael Latil. 36: New Market Battlefield Park, Hall of Valor Museum, copied by Michael Latil. 37: VMI Archives, Lexington, copied by Michael Latil.

38: Courtesy Nick Picerno copied by Bernie Lashua(2) — National Archives Neg. No. 111-B-305. 41: Courtesy Bob Walter, photographed by Mike Walter. 43: Library of Congress. 44, 45: From *The Cavalry*, Vol. 4 of *The Photographic History of the Civil War*, edited by Francis Trevelyan Miller, published by The Review of Reviews Co., New York, 1911 — Painting by Jean-Adolphe Beaucé, Museum of the Confederacy, Richmond, photographed by Katherine Wetzel. 46: Courtesy Bill Turner, copied by Michael Latil. 47: Hagley Museum and Library, Wilmington, Delaware. 48, 49: From *Deeds of Valor*, Vol. 1, edited by W. F. Beyer and O. F. Keydel, published by The Perrien-Keydel Company, Detroit, 1906; National Archives Neg. No. 111-B-3876. 50, 51: Washington and Lee University, The University Library Special Collections, Ellinor Gadsden Papers; Library of Congress. 52: Valentine Museum, Richmond. 54, 55: From *Harper's New Monthly Magazine*; MASS-MOLLUS/USAMHI, copied by A. Pierce Bounds; from *Harper's New Monthly Magazine*, courtesy Frank & Marie-T. Wood Print Collections, Alexandria, Va.(3). 56: Washington and Lee University, The University Library Special Collections, Michael Miley Collection. 58: USAMHI, copied by A. Pierce Bounds. 61: Courtesy of Lynchburg Museum System. 62: Map by William L. Hezlep — Chicago Historical Society Neg. No. ICHi 19830. 63: National Archives Neg. No. 111-B-3913; MASS-MOLLUS/USAMHI, copied by A. Pierce Bounds — National Archives Neg. Nos. 111-B-4593; 165-JT-208; 111-B-4198. 64, 65: Library of Congress. 66, 67: From *The Defenses of Washington, 1861-1865*, by Stanley W. McClure, U.S. Department of the Interior, NPS, National Capital Parks, Reprint, 1961; Library of Congress. 69: Museum of the Confederacy, Richmond, copied by Katherine Wetzel. 70, 71: Painting by William D. Washington, Museum of the Confederacy, Richmond, photographed by Katherine Wetzel. 72: Washington County Historical Society, Hagerstown, Md., photographed by A. Pierce Bounds; West Virginia Department of Culture and History, State Archives. 74: Library of Congress. 75: Sketch by Charles W. Reed, Library of Congress. 76, 77: Courtesy Don Troiani, photographed by Al Freni; courtesy C. Paul Loane, copied by Arthur Soll; The Mariners' Museum, Newport News, Va. 79: Department of Cultural Resources, North Carolina Division of Archives and History — from *Biographies of Representative Women of the South, 1861-1923*, Vol. 2, by Margaret Wootten Collier, published privately,

1923. 80: Map by William L. Hezlep. 81: Painting by Milner Benedict, State Capitol, Office of the Secretary of State, Atlanta, photographed by Michael W. Thomas. 82: From *Deeds of Valor*, Vol. 1, edited by W. F. Beyer and O. F. Keydel, published by The Perrien-Keydel Company, Detroit, 1906. 83: Courtesy Charles E. Ennis; L. M. Strayer Collection, copied by Brian Blauser; courtesy Nick Picerno, copied by Bernie Lashua. 85: Erick Davis Collection, copied by Jeremy Ross — Library of Congress. 87: Drawing by W. E. Ruggles, The Ruggles Collection, University Library, Dundee, Scotland. 88: Courtesy Richard K. Tibbals; California State Capitol Museum, Sacramento, photographed by Robert DiFranco. 90: Courtesy Frank & Marie-T. Wood Print Collections, Alexandria, Va. 91: Courtesy Brian Pohanka; courtesy Nick Picerno, copied by Bernie Lashua. 92, 93: Historical Society of Pennsylvania, inset Kittochtinny Historical Society, Chambersburg, Pa., photographed by A. Pierce Bounds. 94, 95: Minnesota Historical Society; Kittochtinny Historical Society, Chambersburg, Pa., photographed by A. Pierce Bounds — Library of Congress. 96, 97: Library of Congress. 98, 99: Kittochtinny Historical Society, Chambersburg, Pa., copied by A. Pierce Bounds. 101: Courtesy Bob Walter, photographed by Mike Walter. 102: Library of Congress. 105: Courtesy Frank & Marie-T. Wood Print Collections, Alexandria, Va. 106, 107: Painting by H.F.E. Philippoteaux, Museum of the Confederacy, Richmond, photographed by Katherine Wetzel. 108: Courtesy John W. Kuhl; courtesy Don Troiani, photographed by Al Freni. 110, 111: National Archives Neg. No. 111-B-566, inset Library of Congress. 113: Drawings by James E. Taylor, The Western Reserve Historical Society, Cleveland, photographed by Michael McCormick. 114: Drawing by Alfred R. Waud, Library of Congress. 116: Drawing by James E. Taylor, The Western Reserve Historical Society, Cleveland, photographed by Michael McCormick, inset Virginia Historical Society, Richmond. 117: National Archives Neg. No. 111-B-5277; Library of Congress. 118: Map by Walter W. Roberts. 119: Drawing by Alfred R. Waud, Library of Congress. 120, 121: Painting by Thure de Thulstrup, Soldier's and Sailor's Memorial Hall, Pittsburgh, photographed by Herbert K. Barnett. 123: Courtesy Larry B. Williford; courtesy Bill Turner; Library of Congress — drawing by James E. Taylor, The Western Reserve Historical Society, Cleveland, photographed by Michael McCormick. 124, 125: Courtesy Bill Turner — courtesy Frank & Marie-T.

Wood Print Collections, Alexandria, Va. 126: Courtesy Nick Picerno, copied by Bernie Lashua; except top right from *Flags of the Army of the United States Carried during the War of the Rebellion, 1861-1865,* compiled under direction of the Quartermaster General U.S. Army, 1887. 127: R. B. Hayes Presidential Center, HN#566 — Roger D. Hunt Collection/USAMHI, copied by A. Pierce Bounds; courtesy Michael J. McAfee, copied by Bob Monell. 128: From *Flags of the Army of the United States Carried during the War of the Rebellion, 1861-1865,* compiled under direction of the Quartermaster General U.S. Army, 1887 — Russell J. Wunker Collection/USAMHI, copied by A. Pierce Bounds — courtesy Brian Pohanka; The Bennington Museum, Bennington, Vt. 129: Inset courtesy Michael J. McAfee, copied by Bob Monell; Jerry and Teresa Rinker Collection. 130: From *Flags of the Army of the United States Carried during the War of the Rebellion, 1861-1865,* compiled under direction of the Quartermaster General U.S. Army, 1887; from *Album of the Second Battalion Duryee Zouaves,* 1906 — courtesy Michael J. McAfee, copied by Bob

Monell; courtesy Nick Picerno, copied by Bernie Lashua. 131: Courtesy Nick Picerno, copied by Bernie Lashua. 132: From *Flags of the Army of the United States Carried during the War of the Rebellion, 1861-1865,* compiled under direction of the Quartermaster General U.S. Army, 1887 — courtesy C. Paul Loane, copied by Arthur Soll — courtesy Nick Picerno, copied by Bernie Lashua. 133: Courtesy Nick Picerno, copied by Bernie Lashua(2) — courtesy Chris Nelson. 135: Courtesy Seward Osborne, photographed by Henry Groskinsky. 136, 137: Drawings by James E. Taylor, The Western Reserve Historical Society, Cleveland, photographed by Michael McCormick. 138: Drawing by Alfred R. Waud, from *Battles and Leaders of the Civil War,* Vol. 4, published by The Century Co., New York, 1887. 141: Valentine Museum, Richmond (2); courtesy Bill Turner. 142, 143: Courtesy Russ A. Pritchard, photographed by Larry Sherer; Warren Rifles Confederate Museum, photographed by Michael Latil — Museum of the Confederacy, Richmond, photographed by Ronald H. Jennings — Virginia Historical Society, Richmond, photo-

graphed by Ronald H. Jennings — Museum of the Confederacy, Richmond, photographed by Ronald H. Jennings(2); photograph courtesy Bill Turner. 145: Drawing by James E. Taylor, The Western Reserve Historical Society, Cleveland, photographed by Michael McCormick. 146: Drawing by Alfred R. Waud, Library of Congress; courtesy Nick Picerno, copied by Bernie Lashua. 148: Map by Walter W. Roberts and William L. Hezlep. 150: From *History of the Eighth Regiment Vermont Volunteers, 1861-1865,* by George N. Carpenter, published by Press of Deland & Barta, Boston, 1886. 152: Drawing by Alfred R. Waud, Library of Congress. 154, 155: Painting by Julian Scott, Vermont State House, Montpelier, photographed by Henry Groskinsky. 156: Map by Walter W. Roberts and William L. Hezlep. 158: From *Life and Letters of Charles Russell Lowell,* by Edward W. Emerson, published by Houghton, Mifflin and Co., New York, 1907. 159: Courtesy The New-York Historical Society. 160-171: Sketches by James E. Taylor, The Western Reserve Historical Society, Cleveland, photographed by Michael McCormick.

INDEX